a dude's guide to babies

Dedication

This book is dedicated to my mom, who always was sure I could do it, but now will never *know*; to my dad, for showing me how it's done; to my sons, Sarcasmo, Zippy the Monkey Boy, and Hyper Lad, for giving me the reason behind it all; and to She Who Must Be Included in the Dedication, for putting up with most things, encouraging me in the rest, and not minding the names.

—Richard Jones

This book is dedicated to my children. Without them, I would still be the selfish, self-absorbed person I can't stand to be around. To my wife, who does the job of ten people and never complains. To my mother, who instilled in me an attitude that I could always accomplish any goal I set out on. To my great friend and main author, Richard, who gave me the idea for this book by saying, "Dude! There is no guide to babies." And to my father, who taught me that being a great dad does not mean you have to be a "prefect" person.

—Barry Robert Ozer

Published by Sellers Publishing, Inc.

Copyright © 2013 Sellers Publishing, Inc.
Text copyright © 2013 Richard Jones and Barry Robert Ozer
All rights reserved.

Cover image: © Radius Images/Corbis
Cover, interior, and infographic design by Rita Sowins
Photo credits for back cover: (top) Richard Jones photo by Alyse Kelly-Jones, MD; (bottom) Barry Robert Ozer photo by Richard Jones

Sellers Publishing, Inc.
161 John Roberts Road, South Portland, Maine 04106
Visit our Web site: www.sellerspublishing.com • E-mail: rsp@rsvp.com

ISBN 13: 978-1-4162-0889-1
e-ISBN: 978-1-4162-0903-4
Library of Congress Control Number: 2012945288

The information in this book is not meant to replace the guidance of your healthcare providers. Always consult your pediatrician about your baby's health, and your physician about your personal health.

10 9 8 7 6 5 4 3 2
Printed and bound in China.

a dude's guide to babies

• • • • • • • • • • • • • • • • • • • •

THE NEW DAD'S PLAYBOOK

RICHARD JONES & BARRY ROBERT OZER

SELLERS
PUBLISHING

Contents

1 For Rookie Dads   6

2 Name That Dude   13

3 Getting Pregnant   19

4 What's Up, Doc?   46

5 Making the Cut?   56

6 Hold Him Like a Football, but Be Careful
Not to Spike Him   62

7 Safety First, the Dude's Way   66

8 The Inside Scoop on Poop   90

9 Turn and Face the Change . . .   95

10 'S Not a Pretty Sight   108

11 Let Sleeping Babies Lie   112

12 You-Haul . . . a Lot   124

13 The Naked Truth About
Baby Skin   132

14 Mommy Magnet   136

15 Clothes Make the Baby   140

16 Daddy Day Care   143

17 Up for Grabs   152

18 You Scream, I Scream (Not)   155

19 Stuff You've Got to Have   167

20 Splish, Splash, I Was Takin' a Bath   170

21 Things That Go Burp in the Night   175

22 Hitting for the Cycle   188

23 Delegate, Schmelegate   199

24 All Pooped Out   204

Infographic   207
Acknowledgments   208

1

for rookie dads

what to *really* expect after all those months of expecting . . .

Dudes, nobody warned us what it was going to be like when we became dads. Nobody took us aside, knuckled our heads, and whispered the secrets of being a father. It was a shock like no other the first time we were left alone with our kids. We were lost, out to sea, up to our necks in it.

Well, we survived and our kids survived, so we're here to pass along a little of that hard-won wisdom. Okay, not exactly wisdom, more like experience disguised as wisdom, but that counts, right?

So, why did *we* decide to write a book? After all, there are thousands of books about baby rearing written by well-respected folks with actual postgraduate degrees and even abbreviations after their names. We're just two dudes with seven kids between us — Barry's two boys and two girls, and Richard's three boys. We're sure our wives helped somewhere in there, but it gets a bit lost in all the memories of crying and screaming. Oh, and the noises our kids made, too. We survived without any major injuries. To us. We don't have formal educations in child rearing and we didn't attend school to learn anything really useful. However, we do have a lot of experience and a rather different perspective than most of those other authors of books about bringing up babies.

Since most of the books we read had us snoring by the third paragraph, we decided that we needed to write the book we wished we'd had when we first became dads.

Back then, we wanted straight talk. We wanted practical advice. We wanted it all to be wrapped up in a package that was funny enough to keep us interested and short enough to finish quickly so we could catch a few minutes of the game before the baby woke up. In brief, we wanted something we could read on the can.

A Dude's Guide to Babies was born from a panicked conversation between Richard and Barry. Richard, the wily veteran with three little dudes, was trying to console Barry, who'd just gone from DINK (double income, no kids) to adoptive dad of four in the blink of six months.

Barry had traveled through fear, past panic, and out the other side of world-devouring, end-of-life-as-we-know-it terror, emerging in a state of brittle calm. It was a bit nerve-racking for onlookers, who tiptoed gently around Barry, worrying that his inevitable explosion would leave some appalling stains.

So, one day Richard went over to Barry's house to see the sweet little dudette who had just joined Barry's family. She was still wet behind the ears from her birth and had come to live with her brothers and sister under the loving roof provided by Barry and his wife.

Barry's wife is a pediatrician, which meant Barry was going to stay at home for a while to make sure his youngest daughter was taken care of. Barry, a confident serial entrepreneur who felt like he knew more than enough about everything and could always act decisively while being better dressed than the dude in the next cubicle, answered the door on his knees. Metaphorically, if not literally.

His hair was greasy and uncombed. There were stains on his grubby grey sweatshirt and it looked as if his sweatpants were on backwards. To put it bluntly, Barry was a mess.

"Help," he croaked.

Richard walked in, closed the door, and cooed at the cute little dudette in the bassinet by the kitchen table, which was cluttered with dirty dishes from a half-eaten breakfast. He scootched a couple of pairs of shoes off the bench seat, looked into Barry's tired, bloodshot eyes, and tried to be gentle.

"You look terrible," Richard said. "Here's what's going to happen. I'm going to stay here with your beautiful daughter, and you're going to clean yourself up. Take a nice, long shower. Dry off and get dressed. Take your time. When you come back out here, I want to see Barry, not a walking lump of ambulatory clothing held together by sweat and grease and wearing a Barry mask that doesn't really fit."

That's what Richard said. Or words to that effect. Sometimes Richard is more eloquent in his memories than in reality.

Regardless, Barry toddled off to the shower while Richard fed the little dudette, reveling in that new-baby smell. He smiled, feeling more than a little sense of accomplishment that even though he hadn't burped one of his own kids in over a year, he still had what it took to burp a baby. Too bad he forgot to put the towel on his shoulder first.

Barry eventually came out looking almost human, just about the time that his daughter went to sleep in her bassinet. Barry gazed at her, and a look of pure joy brightened his poor, sleep-deprived face.

Setting the baby monitor down on the table next to the sleeping baby, Richard dragged Barry into the living room.

"I think that was my first shower in three days," Barry said. "I'm just so tired all the time. I can't leave her alone. Who knows what might happen?"

Barry kept looking over Richard's shoulder, staring at the door to the kitchen as if he expected to see some tall, hairy, hulking monster stomp out with his youngest daughter in its arms at any minute. None appeared.

"And there's just so much to do," Barry continued. "I've got to feed the other three before they go off to school and day care. And the dirty dishes are stacking up, and their clothes . . . I don't have time to fold them and get them back into the dressers and closets. The kids are just wearing stuff straight out of the dryer."

Drawing on a deep well of practical experience, and an uncanny ability to make it look like he knew what he was doing, Richard said, "Relax. I know exactly what you're feeling. I was the same way with Hyper Lad. If friends came to visit and even breathed quickly, I'd shush them because I was afraid the noise would wake him up. Remember?"

But Barry just snorted and glanced around for the hulking,

baby-stealing yeti he was sure lurked somewhere close by. "I don't know. . . ." he said. "There's so much stuff I don't know how to do. There's no way I can remember to do everything the books talk about. And they make me feel that if I don't do all this stuff — heck, if I don't *already* know how to do all this stuff — I'm going to be a terrible dad. I don't want to be a terrible dad, but . . ."

"Seriously, dude," Richard said. "Relax. I've got good news. You're already a good dad."

"Bluh?" Barry grunted.

"Here's the deal, dude," Richard said. "Your new daughter is alive and well. She's getting enough food and has a safe place to stay. You're keeping her clean, with no diaper rash or stuff like that. That's it, dude. That's all you have to do to succeed as a good dad. Everything else is gravy. I mean, has anyone ever died because they didn't put away the clean laundry? Or didn't do the dishes? No, of course not."

Barry looked at him kind of fuzzily, as if his brain wasn't quite keeping up with Richard's words.

"Gravy," Richard continued. "Pure gravy. The even better news is gravy's easy to make. And that, dude, is what you're going to do . . . go from being a good dad to being a great one. By the way, the gravy was just a metaphor, so don't start looking for biscuits."

Barry smiled. There were plenty more talks, and more learning on both sides, and more gravy made, but that was the start.

We learned to set our expectations at a more realistic level. We accomplished what needed to be accomplished. Once the little dudes and dudettes were fed and housed and kept clean, that gave us a base to move on from.

As we dug out from under the huge weight of expectations we'd placed on ourselves, we found it was easier and easier to get stuff done. The more we accomplished, the easier it was to do the next thing. Our sense of confidence allowed us to leave the panic behind.

Since then, we've done a lot of thinking and a lot of talking with some mothers, ones who just can't believe a dad is taking care of children, and we've come to a couple of conclusions about taking care of babies. The most basic recommendation we can make is this: Don't panic. The second on is: Just focus on the basics. Once you've got those two things down, you're going to feel better about yourself and about your Dad fu. (Think kung fu, only with more diapers and fewer mystical quests.) Once your Dad fu is strong, it's that much easier to move up the ranks to become the Greatest Dad in the World. And you'll have the mug or tie to prove it.

Note: Before we begin, a quick word about, well, words. Sometimes, we'll mention one gender or another to refer to all babies in general. You'll get the idea, and we'll give you credit for knowing when these terms apply generally and when they apply specifically to a little dude or dudette. Also, we sometimes refer to the woman in a dude's life who's doing all the heavy lifting as his "wife" or "partner." We mean for this book to be as inclusive as possible, and so when you see "wife," feel free to substitute girlfriend, partner, husband, or whatever appellation most closely suits your life. As far as we're concerned, anyone who wants to become the best dad possible is all right with us.

name that dude

a field guide to dads

We're going to get a little picky here and dive into some amateur Linnaean classification.

Linnaeus was the dude who came up with the system that lets us name all the stuff around us. No, not English. It's the whole Latin thing. Where humans are classified, in the short version, as Homo sapiens. Sound familiar?

Well, we're going to do a little of that with you dudes here.

Looking at our friends and various dudes who we just like to follow around and watch (restraining orders notwithstanding), we've managed to divide most dudes who are about to become dads into the following categories.

1. **Dude I'llTakeAnother'un.** (These are extremely scientific-y words here. Do not doubt us.) This is the party dude. The dude who can't seem to remember that he actually gave up a Saturday relatively recently to get married.

   He still goes out with the guys most weekends and some weekdays. To him, having a baby was just another excuse to have a party. The reality still hasn't set in. The party isn't over, but it's now going to include clowns instead of Crown Royal.

2. **Dude NeenerNeenerNeenerICan'tHearYou.** This is the
   dude in denial. Deep denial. You know the whole
   thing about how denial isn't just a river in Egypt?
   (This makes sense when you say it out loud.) Yeah,
   that's him. He's living in that desert surrounding
   denial river.

   He's comfortable. He likes his life and is confident in
   his ability to work with his wife to make sure the
   coming baby won't create too big a change in their
   lives. They'll still go out and do stuff, like that camping
   trip he has planned for two weeks after the due date.

   He's in for a deeply shocking reality check. Richard was
   this guy. He assured everyone who would listen, or even
   those who he could only trap for a few minutes, that his
   life wouldn't change just because he had a tiny ankle biter
   around the house. That stance lasted all of five minutes
   after the proto-Sarcasmo (his first little dude, who went
   on to become the world's most sarcastic son, hence the
   name) arrived at the house and peed on Richard. Things
   will change, but it's up to you to determine how much.

3. **Dude LateNightAtTheOffice.** This is your typical, type A,
   hard-charging, give-it-his-all-and-then-a-little-more,
   pride-of-his-boss, worker dude. He not only defines
   himself by his job, he literally can't imagine himself doing
   anything else. If he isn't giving all his time to his work, he
   feels like he's slacking off.

   He's determined not to let his baby become a distraction.
   Not that it will be, of course, because he's scheduled
   some quality baby time for the seventeenth from 4:10

through 4:27 p.m., just before the Rogers-account Skype call. Hee, hee, hee. This is the one who really cracks us up. Scheduling and babies go together like chocolate and onions. With your little dude or dudette, it will take an hour just to run a single errand, so get ready to embrace this fact: from now on, scheduling is something that happens to other people.

4. **Dude StuckToTheCouchus.** We've all seen this dude. Or, Richard said, looking snarkily at Barry, been this dude at one time or another. This is the type of dude who does just enough to get by and then no more. After all, any more and he'd have to actually get up off the couch, and that might allow the comfy lumps in the cushions, contoured to his body, to lose their shape. That would be bad.

This dude gets cranky if he doesn't get his nine hours of solid sleep every single night. That alone is enough to guarantee a sincerely nasty wake-up once the baby arrives in the house. As we'll say elsewhere, baby stomachs are very, very, very tiny, so they can't hold all that much milk. Which means they're up and hungry every couple of hours. And while their stomachs haven't developed, we certainly can't say the same for their lungs.

Here's the thing. Each and every one of these types of dudes are about to see a major paradigm shift in their lives. All of them manifest their self-centeredness in a different way, but it's always all about them. Their wants, their needs.

That will not stand. Once the little dude or dudette pops out into the world, your life will find a brand-new focus, one that requires constant supervision, attention, and worry. Constantly.

16

A new baby doesn't leave you enough time to keep all your focus on yourself. It's hard to keep staring at yourself in the mirror when you've got to train both eyes on the little dude in the crib.

No matter what kind of dude you are, get ready for your life to change once the little bundle of spit and joy makes his or her initial appearance. Change isn't half so scary when you know it's coming, because you can get ready to work with the change, rather than fight against it.

What kind of dude are you? So overprotective you're the Black Hawk version of the helicopter dad? Or so laid-back you're not even sure that childproofing your home means more than locking the front door? If you're way too . . . overbearing . . . with your first child, don't worry — you'll loosen up by the time your second one comes on the scene. If you've been a little too . . . relaxed . . . with dude number one, no problem — you'll learn soon enough how to be more attentive to any of the other little dudes or dudettes who may come along afterward.

Richard swears the following isn't true, but anecdotal evidence says he's being willfully blind to this evolution. Sarcasmo, the oldest child of Richard and his wife, waddled through a babyproofed environment that was so safe, the little dude almost choked to death on the cushions plastering every surface below three feet. Zippy the Monkey Boy, the middle child, liked to climb and did so with great alacrity, easily clambering up trees and only upsetting his parents when he got high enough that they couldn't climb up to get him. Five years later, when Hyper Lad came along, things had really loosened up. Dropped binkies didn't get sterilized, they got wished off. As in, "I wish this were cleaner, but oh well. . . ." Hyper Lad wasn't really allowed to juggle the kitchen knives — it just looked that way that one time.

So, yeah, it's something that will happen to you. You will be more strict with your first child. You will make mistakes.

We mean, it's not like there's some kind of funny, short, (semi) well-researched guide to help you out or anything.

ahem

Even if there were such a guide, you'd still be making mistakes. It's what humans do. We have to see things for ourselves. Get used to the idea.

Just don't settle is all we're asking. You have to learn from your mistakes. Don't beat up on yourself when they happen, and try not to take yourself quite so seriously as you learn to be a dad. When you have a decision to make, concerning something you know is going to come up again later in your little dudette's extensive therapy sessions, try asking yourself a little question: Is this really cause for alarm, or is it just me overreacting?

Answer that question, and we think you'll be on your way to doing right by your firstborn.

Just so you know, Richard was a firstborn and knows that every word of this is true. He had to break parental ground for his younger sister, Tia, on everything. She got it easy, even if she won't admit it. Barry, who wasn't a firstborn, vehemently disagrees that the older child makes things easier for the younger ones. He says that it was hard for every child in his family, but he's willing to admit that he might be wrong. He's definitely the bigger man.

3

getting pregnant

see one. do one. teach one.

Congratulations, dude.

No, really. We mean it. Congratulations. You are the best (eastern district codirector of sales remediation/cook/writer/ salesman/bureaucrat/delivery dude/mad scientist/pilot/ store-window-mannequin dresser) in your company.

You are the go-to dude. You *know* what to do, when to do it, and how it can be done the best way possible. You *know*.

Any problem that gets thrown your way is just another opportunity for you to show off the skillz that pay your billz. (Sorry. Sometimes the urge to pretend we're actually somewhat cool overwhelms us.)

Anyway. What we're actually saying is that while you might know exactly what you're doing at work, that very particular set of skills and knowledge doesn't exactly translate into helping you take care of a poopy diaper or force a huge burp.

Don't despair, though. We're not saying you're some sort of incompetent drone, incapable of doing the work a dad needs to do. We're not saying you should just give up and let your wife do all the baby work.

Not at all.

We just want you to take the time to ask for help when you don't actually know what you're supposed to be doing. It's a hard thing to do, asking for help. To a lot of dudes, asking for help (or directions) is a sign of weakness, as if not knowing how to do everything, or how to get absolutely anywhere, is a personality defect, as opposed to just the way things are.

In fact, asking "how" is a vital part of the process of turning book-stuffed young medical-school graduates into actual doctors who won't frighten you into sprinting from the examining table and out into traffic. There's a saying in medical residency that covers this need to ask for help so you can learn: See one. Do one. Teach one.

Sure, it's a bit optimistic, but it's a great template to follow. You see an expert (someone who was changing the diapers on her dolls since she was four) change a diaper. Then, working under the expert's supervision (say, for example, your wife's eagle-eyed, gimlet stare as you touch *her* baby that *she* carried inside *her* womb for nine months and don't you forget it), you actually go ahead and change a diaper. Finally, once you're sure you know what you're doing (in a limited sense), you teach a fellow dude how to change the diaper. In all seriousness, nothing helps you learn a skill like trying to teach it to someone else.

See one. Do one. Teach one. Words to live by. And to put into practice, as the following story makes clear.

> **Richard:** *My friend Delton and I grew up and went to high school together. But then our paths diverged; when I went off to the University of Florida, Delton stayed in Texas and attended Texas Tech.*

When I had little dudes, Delton decided he had to have another beer. When I got married and got a job, Delton got another beer and a coozie to keep it cold longer.

Parenting, to Delton, was something foreign, something so very different it might as well have been some esoteric mating dance on the planet Hngtrnkb 3. In other words, it was totally out of his comfort zone.

So he looked on my oldest little dude, the baby who would one day come to be called Sarcasmo, and saw not a loving bundle of cuteness and joy, but an alien object with mysterious needs and dubious penchants that caused Delton to want to grab another Bud. Still, Delton is the sort to try anything once. And things that didn't actively repel him or result in some involuntary reverse peristalsis, he'd try twice. He wasn't sure how one went about taking care of a baby, but he was willing to learn. At least that's what Delton kept telling me.

"Tell you what," Delton said in his thick, Texas accent (which makes it difficult for me to believe that he earns his living as a lawyer). "Next time he dirties his diaper, why don't you let me take care of it?"

Well, the idea of Delton being in charge of cleaning my fragile little boy, the light of my life, the fruit of my seed, etc., etc., was more than frightening. I wasn't worried about the future Sarcasmo. I was worried about the possible damage to Delton's psyche when he attempted to go where he'd never gone before.

Delton, though, assured me that he was not only willing,

he was ready and excited to try something new. Little dudes being little dudes, Delton got his chance just a short while later.

After we left the local diner, I spread out the changing mat on a nearby bench, gently placed the baby on it — making sure there was enough room on either side that he wasn't in immediate danger of falling off (although I still made sure to hold onto him with a firm but gentle grip) — and nodded to Delton that it was time.

He looked up at me with a frown on his face.

"All right," he drawled. "How do I pop the top on this puppy?"

I walked him through unsnapping the little dude's onesie and rolling it up around his chest. Then we had to go step by step on how to remove a diaper without getting the contents all over the remover and the removee. Which was just about the time that the little dude decided to add a little something extra to the proceedings. Delton suddenly swayed on the bench, turned an unfamiliar shade of green, and lifted his gaze from the rapidly swelling, partially opened diaper.

Shaking his head, Delton muttered, "A man's got to know his limitations. We just passed mine. I think I'm gonna leave this one to the experts."

Delton was, and is, a smart dude.

Look at what he did. He asked what to do when he didn't know the next step. He actually listened to the instructions and followed them. Most important, when he knew he couldn't do something, he stepped aside rather than bulling his way through and mucking up the job.

When the project you're working on is a young life for which you are responsible, doing a half-assed job isn't going to cut it. It's all right if you don't know how to do something, as long as you use that as an opportunity to learn. It's all right to ask directions, as long as you actually follow them. You can't learn without asking, and you can't remember without doing.

Think of your first few years with your little dude or dudette as going back to school, only this time you'll get a poop-filled diaper at the end instead of a square hat with a tassel attached. That sounds like a fair trade to us.

"You're What???"

Easily, and by a very large margin, one of the biggest shocks to get over is when your wife or girlfriend tells you she's pregnant.

> **Barry:** *I wouldn't know. We adopted. But Rick's wife is going to kill him for this next bit. . . .*

> **Richard:** *I do know about that shock. It's true. Brother, it is true.*

We've talked to hundreds of dudes out there, and every single one of them felt the same way. Most described the feeling of learning they were going to be fathers as something like getting an axe handle to the back of their heads. It didn't matter if they had been trying to get pregnant for years, trying for days, or not even trying. When a woman walks up to you, smiles, and says, "I'm pregnant," it's one helluva shock.

Now, here's a bit of crucial advice: When she tells you she's pregnant, you need to get over that shock so quickly she'll never even know it was there.

In fact, start practicing right now. Go find a poker game (live, not online) and start playing. Master the best poker face at the table. Learn to stare down hissing cobras — anything that will help you to never show shock on your face. The mother of your baby-to-be will not appreciate gape-jawed stupor on your mug.

> **Richard:** *Trust me on that one. Appreciation will not be a word in her vocabulary should you not do a credible job of disguising the jolt of terror bouncing around in your brain. Her vocabulary will instead consist of very short words, all of which have something to do with inflicting severe pain.*

You'll have plenty of time to digest the news later. The first thing you need to do is trot out your biggest smile, your happiest voice, and your twinkliest eyes, and don't stop hugging her.

We're not really saying you should fake anything. We're just suggesting that you speed up your natural reactions pretty darn quickly. Why? We're going to do a little stereotyping here, but we've found it to be true. Pregnant women are (well, only sometimes, you understand) a teensy bit emotional, and shock can easily be mistaken for dismay. And that is not the way you want to start out on your nine-month adventure in gestation.

Even if she doesn't say anything at the time, she'll remember that you weren't instantly as happy as she was, and *that*, friends, will come back to haunt you.

So, since we all want a household of harmony, peace, and joy all the time, and especially during those emotional months of pregnancy, it's best to do your part right from the start. Once the initial celebrations are over, and you've hugged and kissed and jumped up and down, wait until you've got a little time to yourself to uncork your emotions and realize just what you're in for. Call a fellow dude, preferably one who's already been through all this. Most likely, he'll know exactly how you're feeling and will help you deal with all your fears so they don't get out of control.

We recommend trying to get a little "you time" in those early days, so you can wrestle any doubts into submission and get ready to support her as much as possible as her body goes through changes your puberty never thought of, not even on its worst days.

Double-Secret Probation

Obviously, the first thing you're going to want to do is shout to the heavens about your mighty seed finding purchase, but that's really not the best idea.

You see, more than 30 percent of pregnancies end in a miscarriage during the first trimester. Up to 80 percent of all miscarriages occur in the first trimester. (Pregnancies are divided into first, second, and third trimesters, each lasting three months.) After the first trimester, if everything's going fine with the baby and the mom, it's a lot less likely that there will be a miscarriage. Which is why obstetricians (doctors who deal with pregnancy and childbirth) often recommend that you not tell anyone about the pregnancy until after the first trimester.

The reason's pretty simple. Losing a pregnancy is pretty traumatic for both the mother and the father, and, if they're like most people, they'll want to grieve in private. Imagine that you've already told everyone you know that you're going to have a baby. Now, imagine the worst happens and she miscarries. After that, imagine calling back everyone you just told about the baby and having to now tell them that the baby died.

No. Not something you want to do. At all.

And besides, isn't it exciting to have a secret that only the two of you know? Being able to drop little hints into conversation that no one but she will get? You betcha.

Ice Cream and Pickles

There's this myth about pregnancy that says when a woman is pregnant, she's going to start craving very strange things, like, for instance, a big dill pickle smothered in mint chocolate-chip ice cream. Like a lot of myths, cravings are both true and false.

The ice-cream-and-pickles bit may be true for some women,

but not for most of them. In fact, cravings, if they happen at all, will be different for each woman. The reason is, once again, those wacky hormones running like crazy through her body.

Those hormones are causing changes in your partner's sense of taste and smell. That's why she may be looking for different food combinations. Most women who have cravings say that sweets and dairy products are on the top of their list, as well as sour fruits and spicy foods.

Barry: *If I had a choice, I'd prefer the sex cravings!*

Crackers

Here's another fun bit about pregnancy: morning sickness. This little biological gem is thought to be caused by way too much estrogen running riot through a woman's body. Basically, morning sickness can strike at any time: it results in a woman waking up in the morning and rushing to the bathroom to vomit up whatever's in her stomach. The good news is that for most women, it usually vanishes sometime after the first trimester.

You might wish morning sickness were a myth, but, dude, it's not. So, when it happens to your wife or partner, don't just lie there in the bed, wishing she'd get it over with quickly so you can go back to sleep. Get your lazy butt up, go in there, and help, whether that means holding her hair out of the way, getting a wet towel to wipe her mouth, or just rubbing her back. Show her that you can be there for her. Unless she's told you she'd rather be alone, do not roll over and pretend to sleep through it. She'll know. And don't run around panicking and asking, "What do I do? What do I do?"

Just remember high school and college hangovers. Get her some water and just be there.

Which reminds us of another important truism about makin' babies. Pregnancy is not something that just happens to her. When she's pregnant, so are you . . . we're fully aware that we don't have a clue what's it's really like to go through the physical stuff — we don't have to carry and pass a bowling ball through a rather small orifice. But we do know what it's like to be there for her emotionally. And if *we* can do it, dude, so can you.

Most of those fancy books recommend that, to fight morning sickness, women should lie still in bed and then eat some dry crackers before getting up. That's probably a pretty good idea, even if you have to brush cracker crumbs out of the bed. If it stops her from throwing up, isn't that worth a few crumbs on the sheet and blanket?

"I Look Like I'm What?"

Morning sickness, unfortunately, isn't confined to just the morning. In fact, with some women, it continues throughout the day and severely affects their appetite. Which means there could be a lot of food left over on her plate.

We know you'll be tempted, but, dude, don't eat it. You will regret it.

For a lot of dudes, pregnancy means that not only will she be getting bigger, but so will they. If their wife or girlfriend doesn't eat, many dudes will gorge on her leftovers. If their wife or girlfriend is eating like there's no tomorrow, then a lot of dudes will start to match her plate for plate.

Either way, there's every possibility that you'll gain just as much weight as she does. Too bad for the dudes that they don't lose anything at the end of the pregnancy. It sticks around, and when we say around, we mean, you know, round.

Richard: *Don't ask. Just don't ask.*

No, Do Ask

When we say you should ask, we're suggesting that you ask any questions you have of a very specific person, someone you didn't know a year ago. Basically, what we're recommending is that you attend as many visits as possible when your wife or girlfriend goes to the obstetrician. Sure, there's going to be some icky stuff discussed, some things you'd probably rather not know, but knowledge is power. The more you know about what's happening during the pregnancy and what will happen during the birth, the less freaked out you'll get.

If you do have questions, you ought to write them down on an index card or something small you can slip into your pocket. That way you can carry them around, and you'll have them ready the next time you see the doctor.

Don't worry about being overly inquisitive. Obstetricians *love* getting questions (we know this for a fact; we've talked to lots of them, and Richard is married to one). In the next chapter, we'll cover in more detail what kinds of questions you should be asking your potential/actual obstetrician, so try to hold on until then. It's not that long a wait. Or you can just skip ahead, then come back. We'll wait.

As for the rest of you, who didn't go haring off into the unknown but decided to stay with us and use the correct route, we've got a few words about . . .

A Package for You

All those weeks of pain and worry and joy and overeating when your wife doesn't even nibble at her dinner. . . . will ultimately lead to one big moment: a very special delivery.

We're sure you dudes have seen this before. The wife wakes up the husband and tells him, "It's time." She's in labor. And he completely loses his sh— stuff. Runs around screaming and panicking and then charges out into the night to race to the hospital, forgetting only one thing: yeah, the mother-to-be.

You don't want to be that dude.

Which means you're going to have to do a little advance planning. We know, not a specialty, but you can do this. One thing all the pregnancy books talk about is making sure you have a "go bag" packed, ready and waiting by the door leading to your car. And that is one very, very good idea.

If you start working on the go bag a couple of months before your due date, you've got plenty of time to futz around with the contents, maybe adding something you read about, maybe taking out the aromatherapy spritzer or whatever you deem a bit too much.

While the full list is up to you, we've come up with a list of *the* ten things you must have in your go bag if you want to get through the delivery reasonably intact.

the dude's guide top 10 list of things you need for the delivery

1. a change of clothing and basic hygiene products for you and the new mom

2. a favorite blanket or pillow

3. insurance cards, pre-filled-out hospital forms, and lots of change for the vending machines

4. a couple of good movies for both of you to watch in case her labor pains slow down

5. a strip of leather for her to put between her teeth when the contractions really start to come on strong (a sense of humor will get you through a lot)

6. something in the colors you both have chosen (perhaps orange and blue?) for your new little dude or dudette to wear home

7. a dedicated video camera (if your hospital allows this) or still camera (a smartphone probably will do in a pinch, but we're of the opinion that single-use gadgets just work better than the multifunction smartphone).

8. a list of who you want to notify after the big moment

9. a maternity bra with nursing pads and warm socks for her, because there's nothing worse than being in a hospital and having cold feet, all other things being equal

10. an iPod with external speakers so she can listen to the music of her choice when she tries to focus on anything other than the extreme pain of the next contraction

As a special treat, we're not going to provide you with pictures of an actual delivery. For those of you who haven't already gone through a delivery, we don't want to spoil the surprise — and if we show you a sneak preview, you won't have that "ohmygod" face when the moment arrives, and where's the funny without that?

We are, however, going to give you a little insight into what an actual delivery can be like. All without having to wear that silly scrub hat. Read on.

"Houston, We Have Splashdown" or What's Messy and Bloody and Very, Very Loud?

This is it, dude. The Big Moment. When you step out of the on-deck circle and into the batter's box, to have something screaming thrown at you, at 100 miles per hour.

Delivery. The birth. The big splat. The drop-off. The drive-by. The catch.

Call it what you will, but this is The Ultimate Event. This is the one that marks the end of expecting things, and the beginning of experiencing things. It's a wonderful, beautiful adventure, complete with a lot of screaming and yelling and panic and blood. And some of that comes from the baby.

But let's back up just a bit here, dudes, and talk about a few of the possibilities.

Birth, contrary to what our parents told us, doesn't occur when the stork flies by and tucks a little baby under a leaf in the cabbage patch. Babies come into the world in different ways, and all of them involve a lot more mess than you might have been anticipating.

To begin with, there are two ways you can start getting into the whole birthing thing. One way is that your doctor might induce labor. This usually occurs when the doctor feels that waiting any longer for the baby to make his first appearance on his own time might be a bad thing for the baby or the mom-to-be.

The reasons for an induction are many. One of them could be that your wife's term is beyond 42 weeks. Forty weeks is the nine months of legend. Most doctors will induce labor if the little dude decides to stay inside for two additional weeks. At around that time, it's all about getting the little dude out and into the world.

An induction normally is scheduled in advance, anywhere from a couple of days to a couple of weeks (or more) before the procedure takes place. There's plenty of time to pack up the bags, make sure you've got everything you need (including the mom-to-be), panic, quash the panic, panic some more, and then drive very sedately to the hospital.

The worst part is that you don't get to go screaming into the ambulance bay, or jump out of the car, race into the ER, and holler for a wheelchair. So you lose out on that bit of fun, but, on the plus side, you do have much less chance of a car accident.

If your little dudette doesn't need to be induced to come out, that means she's going to come out on her own. We're going to assume everything is healthy and going well on the inside, so we'll talk about how she'll probably start knocking on the door somewhere around 40 weeks.

Or so.

That "or so" is pretty important. Because it means that your wife can go into labor at any time. Let us repeat that: At. Any. Time.

There are 24 hours in a day. We sleep about eight of them.

So we're awake for twice as many hours as we are asleep. You'd think the odds of labor starting and the baby coming when you're normally awake would be twice as big.

But you'd be wrong. Because getting awakened by a sudden death grip on your upper arm, and opening your eyes to see a straining and scared face when your brain is still several hours from being capable of handling anything more complex than saying "Ugh". . . well, that's just a lot funnier. And life has a vicious sense of humor.

Which means the odds are you're going to be awakened in a panic by your wife, who's just gone into labor when it's so dark outside that even shadows are turning on night lights.

The good news is that you don't have to become an expert — just know enough to be supportive. After all, your wife has just spent approximately . . . um . . . her whole life worrying about this sort of thing. She knows when to call the doctor, when to head to the hospital, when the contractions are coming closer together, and how to time them. Working together, the two of you will be able to pull this off without any sitcom shenanigans.

> **Richard:** *When we had our second son, my wife woke me up at 3 a.m. so I could time her contractions. She really expected me to be able to do that, and I didn't want to disappoint her.*
>
> *She'd say one was starting. I'd look at the time and then fall instantly back to sleep. She'd say the contraction was over, and I'd do some quick calculations to tell her how long it lasted. And then I'd fall instantly asleep.*

She'd wake me up to tell me another contraction had begun. More math. I'd tell her how long it was between contractions.

Rinse. Repeat.

Apparently, I'm pretty good at pretending to know what I'm doing while I'm half asleep.

Eventually, contractions will progress to the point where she is ready to call the doctor and receive the go-ahead to get to the hospital for the big moment.

You'll be in charge of gathering up the go bag full of essentials, escorting your wife to the car, and doing the driving. We have some special advice for those of you who try to cover your nervous feelings by making bad jokes. Like a certain someone speaking in the plural voice here. Not that we're naming names, are we, Richard? Anyway, if you're that type, our most important piece of advice is: Don't. Just don't. Don't make jokes. Don't try to be funny. Be silent or supportive or both. Do not make jokes. She will not find anything funny, so don't try.

Once you make it to the hospital and endure all the fun with getting admitted and signing on the dotted line and initialing here and initialing there and signing over there, and don't forget the back of the form, too, you'll head up to the room reserved for you.

Don't panic if it seems like a decorator's trunk exploded in the room. Putting frills on delicate, sensitive, and expensive medical equipment is standard practice.

After getting settled in, labor will continue to progress.

There are a lot of ways things can go from here. Your wife might decide to get some medicine to help deal with the pain. Normally, this is an epidural, which means an anesthesiologist comes in and sticks a needle close to your wife's spinal cord and then starts dripping anesthetic in there.

Make sure you have a camera handy. Your wife's blissed-out smile is something you're going to want to capture.

Or she might decide to go the natural way. In which case, the best way for her to cut her pain is by giving some of it to you. Know all those television shows where the woman in labor starts grabbing her husband and yelling obscenities? That's all real. Just grin and bear it. Consider it your down-payment on not having an 8-pound child squeezed out of your nether quarters. Yeah, we thought it might be easier to take all the screaming directed right at you, once you considered it that way.

If the labor progresses satisfactorily, and your wife's cervix thins out and dilates to 10 centimeters, everything's going great, and you're going to have a baby delivered by the vaginal method. That is, the baby's going to get pushed out of your wife's vagina.

Just to give you fair warning: this will get messy. There will be blood and liquids and stuff, but you need to man up. Nature, red in tooth and claw, isn't always pretty, but it does have some very nice payoffs.

If your wife's labor doesn't progress satisfactorily, then

the doctor probably will recommend that your wife gets a Cesarean section (often shortened to C-section). That's when the doctor will operate on your wife to remove the baby surgically. If you're in the operating room with her (and we recommend you be there), you're going to be positioned near your wife's head.

The good news is that you'll be on the safe side of the curtain the medical pros will erect so your wife doesn't see what's going on during the surgery. If you listen to no other piece of advice in this book, listen to this. Do. Not. Look. On. The. Other. Side. Of. The. Curtain.

Trust us on this. Just don't.

> **Richard:** *Though our first child was delivered by C-section, we were lucky to have our second come out all on his own, a vaginal birth (also known as VBAC, vaginal birth after Cesarean). Our third little dude was induced, but not because he was late. We were about to move to Charlotte, North Carolina, and we needed to have the baby before then. Everything went smoothly once the induction started. As it progressed, my wife looked at me and asked, quite confident that I would refuse, if I wanted to deliver the baby. Because I wanted to see the look on her face when I confounded her expectations, and also because I tend not to think things through, I said yes.*
>
> *That's how it came to be that I was the one who actually delivered Hyper Lad. Before the big moment, our obstetrician pulled me aside and told me everything I would need to know. "First," he said, "put on these*

*scrubs. You can't do this if you don't look official."
Hearing my wife grunt in pain and knowing my moment
to shine was coming, I was a bit more nervous than I
thought I would be. I managed to fall twice while trying
to put on the scrub pants.*

*Once I was dressed like a fake doctor — or, more
accurately, like a dad who was in so far over his head
he didn't even know there was a surface — the doctor
sat me down and gave me a crash course in delivering a
baby, condensing four years of medical school and four
years of obstetrical residency into a five-minute lecture.
I was impressed.*

*Yep, I was impressed, right up until I was standing there,
staring at the top of a baby's head protruding out into
the world. Still, the lecture was simple enough. Gently
grasp the head and then pull down and out, making sure
you're ready to catch the rest of the body. Which I did.*

*I still can't believe I actually went through with it and
managed to pull it off without anyone getting injured,
but, dude, I'm glad I did. If you get a chance, I'd say give
it a shot. As a dad, it's a rare and very cool thing to be
the first person to see and hold your newborn baby.*

By the way, if your new child is a little dude, you need to be
prepared for this: when he first comes out, he's going to have
a simply enormous set of testicles on him. Seriously, they're
going to be huge.

Relax. It doesn't mean he's going to go through life with a
pair of cantaloupes between his legs. It's simply a natural

reaction to the trauma his little body just went through. In a short while, the testicles will shrink down to their normal, baby-boy size.

Even Dudes Get the Blues

Time to shift gears a little bit here, dudes. We want to talk about a very real problem that hasn't been getting all that much attention.

You've probably heard of the "baby blues," a general feeling of malaise in women following childbirth, or its much more severe cousin, postpartum depression. At its worst, postpartum depression (also know as postnatal depression) can lead to women taking their own lives and the lives of their children. This is something that should definitely be taken seriously.

Traditionally, women who experience postpartum depression are more likely to look and feel sad, and to have difficulty bonding with their new baby. The actress Brooke Shields was brave enough to write about her own postpartum depression in her book, *Down Came the Rain*: ". . . this was sadness of a shockingly different magnitude [than PMS]. It felt as if it would never go away." It's known that this condition affects many new mothers. What's not as well known is the fact that lots of men are affected by postpartum depression, too — about one in ten new dads, according to a study published in *The Journal of the American Medical Association* in May 2010. Apparently, the risks peak when the new baby is between three and six months old. To us, that's a significant number of guys at risk for depression.

It's understandable. You've been focusing on a big, huge event for more than nine months, and it's finally happened. There's bound to be some letdown. In addition, you've now got to care for a newborn, which, shock of all shocks, is a lot of work and makes a significant impact on the way you live your life.

For most dudes, postpartum depression is going to be expressed differently than it is among women. The study found that men are more likely to express their depression by becoming irritable and angry, and by withdrawing from their family. The authors of the study call these behaviors "red flags," and urge family members to keep on the lookout for them. So, yeah, depression is a very real possibility during what should be one of the happiest times in your life.

We're not saying that this is going to happen to you, but it could. It's something you need to consider and keep an eye out for. You're probably not the best person to gauge whether or not you're getting irritable and withdrawn, but do keep an ear out in case folks tell you that you've been . . . "acting differently" . . . lately.

The good news is that there is help, and you are not alone. Mental-health professionals have become adept at treating depression, and specifically postpartum depression. To get help, all you have to do is ask. You're not the only dad to experience this, nor will you be the last. But you are the only you around, so make sure you're the best you.

● ● ●

Whenever we told dudes about this section of the book, we almost always got the same reaction. They would laugh — loudly — until we assured them that this was a real thing, and we were going to write about it in the *Dude's Guide*.

And then they got real quiet. "That's a real thing?" they asked.

"Yeah," we told them. "It's a real thing, and it even has a name: paternal postpartum depression."

"So," they said, with a sigh that was almost like relief, "it wasn't just me."

We were surprised to find out that this is one of those big unspokens — the kind of condition men try to shrug off, if they even go so far as to tell anybody else about it. That's why the findings published in *The Journal of the American Medical Association* are so important. James F. Paulson, Ph.D., from the Eastern Virginia Medical School, and Sharnail D. Bazemore conducted the research, and they provide some helpful advice, which was reported by Rick Nauert, Ph.D., in PsychCentral.com.

"There are many implications of these findings," they wrote. "The observation that expecting and new fathers disproportionately experience depression suggests that more efforts should be made to improve screening and referral, particularly in light of the mounting evidence that early paternal depression may have substantial emotional, behavioral, and developmental effects on children."

One of the most striking findings is that if one parent is suffering from postpartum depression, the other one may be, too. A new dad may be reluctant to speak about his feelings of depression if he knows his wife is having these feelings, too. He may not want to burden her. For that reason, the researchers state that "prevention and intervention efforts for depression in parents might be focused on the couple and family rather than the individual."

A major problem for men with postpartum depression is their sense of isolation. Many depressed new fathers think they're the only ones going through this, and that they have no one to turn to. As we've mentioned, they aren't alone. And support is as close as their phone. Researchers have found that even venting to a friend about the difficulties of parenting can offer significant relief.

There's nothing to be ashamed of if you have paternal postpartum depression. Having a new baby is *hard*. Your sleep rhythm gets destroyed. There's the extra responsibility, and you may be feeling challenging emotions you've never felt before. Getting depressed and not doing anything about it is only going to hurt you in the long run.

If you think you might be depressed, talk to your doctor. Or your buds. Or your wife. Just talk to someone. Remember, this isn't a laughing matter.

Toughing it out is only going to make things tougher on you. We all need a hand, but it's only the ones who ask for that help who can benefit from it.

pop's quiz

It's no secret that some people weren't cut out to be dads. We know you're not one of them. After all, you're already reading from the Font of All Wisdom for Dads.* That shows you're ready to be a dad. The question that's on everybody's mind (most definitely including your little dude and his future hypnotherapist) is what kind of dad are you?

1 Unless you're starring on a reality show broadcast by TLC, the odds of you first finding out about the pregnancy when the baby pops out are pretty slim. You will know you're going to be a dad *before* you become a dad. How do you find out? If you are emptying the trash in your bathroom and notice a box for a pregnancy test, do you. . .

    A. squeal, drop everything, and rush to Walmart to buy as many footballs, baseballs, baseball bats and mitts, basketball goals and balls as you could find?

    B. empty the trash, and then, over dinner, casually ask what's the deal?

    C. gasp, run screaming from the bathroom, and smash your head into the door frame, only to wake up three years later in Chile, speaking Spanish and wondering why everyone calls you Raul?

2 Practice, it's said, makes perfect. There's another saying in the baby-making game about how you've got to practice a lot before you get it right and make the baby. Practice. Mmmmmm. Yeah, a lot of that. So, once the metaphorical rabbit dies, and you realize practice is over and it's time for the game to start, what do you do?

    A. Wonder what all the fuss was about, because, frankly, you were getting a little tired of all that "practice"?

    B. Slowly nod your head and start hoping that women really do get a bit . . . randy . . . later in the pregnancy (they do), all the while telling your wife how glad you are?

    C. Excuse yourself for a moment, go into your bedroom and silently weep over your extensive collection of "libido enhancers" that just arrived in the mail only the day before?

* Okay, we're good, but not that good!

3 **During a dinner out, you notice your wife is oddly happy. You ask her what's up, and she ducks her head, smiles shyly, and says she's pregnant. Which of the following do you do next?**

    A. Squeal, kneel into a perfect Tebow on the floor, jump up loudly while thrusting your fists to the heavens, and begin praising the motility of your "boys" as loudly as possible.

    B. Smile like a fool, take your wife's hand across the table, and tell her you've never been happier and can't wait to see how beautiful she becomes when she's pregnant.

    C. Begin totaling up college costs, indexed to inflation and the consumer price index, adding in a few extras, like braces, because, frankly, you've seen her family picture and there wasn't a straight tooth in the bunch.

If you answered A to these questions, you might want to take a deep breath and try to get calm before you burst a blood vessel somewhere relatively important. You've got 18 more years to go during Basic Fatherhood 101, so you might want to pace yourself a little. If you answered B to these questions, particularly the last one, then, dude, what are you reading this book for? You should be writing your own book. If you answered B to question 3, well, that will be enough to get you through anything. If you answered C to these questions, you're in appalling need of our advanced, intensive program. Go to the back of the book and fill out the entrance form for a crash course as quickly as possible.

4

what's up, doc?

decisions, decisions

Provided everything goes all right during the delivery and your little dudette and wife are doing great, you'll all probably go home in a day or two. (If the delivery is by C-section, your wife may have to stay at the hospital a few days longer.) Raising a child in the wild is rough and requires you to make a lot of decisions every day. One of the decisions that needs to be made way before your bundle of joy arrives at home is who the baby's pediatrician will be. Hey dudes, if your own childhood is a blur, a pediatrician is a doctor who specializes in caring for children from birth to age 18. Give yourself plenty of time to pick a doctor for your little one, since this is one of the most important decisions you'll make.

As you might guess, we've got some suggestions.

- Don't be afraid to ask around. Talk with friends or neighbors who have already had children, and ask whom they would recommend.

- Try to find a pediatrician who is actually nearby. It's not the only thing to consider, but driving for an hour or two just to get to the doctor because your little dude has the sniffles can become a pain in the neck.

- Once you've narrowed your list to a few good doctors, call them up and arrange to have an appointment with them. You and your partner should go in and meet with each of them face to face; seeing whom you're both most compatible with will help you make your decision.

• When you're in each doctor's office, take a little time to look around. Do you like what you see? Is the office spotless or on the messy side? Make sure it looks well run and organized. For instance, one hallmark of an efficient pediatrician's office is that it will have one room for sick kids and one room for those who are well. That way, the well kids don't become the sick kids.

• Also, most doctors are part of group practices. Sometimes, especially in emergency situations, you may be dealing with one of the pediatrician's partners. Meet with them as well, just to have peace of mind that they're also doctors that you'd want treating your child.

• You're going to be spending a lot of time with the office staff, so you need to make sure there's no one there who really rubs you the wrong way. Because, if there is, you just know that's the person you're going to be talking with the most.

top 10 questions to ask prospective doctors

Here's our list of questions you need to get answered before choosing a doctor. This list is not comprehensive, and you should feel free to add any questions of your own.

1. Do you accept our insurance?

2. What days do you work, and is your office open on weekends?

3. What are your hours?

4. Can we meet your partners?

5. If we call with an emergency, whom will we talk to, a doctor or a nurse?

6. To what hospitals do you admit patients?

7. If we have to take our baby to the emergency room, will we see you or another doctor?

8. How long have you been in practice?

9. Are you board certified? (If they are, it means they have passed an exam from the American Academy of Pediatrics and should be well versed in the latest treatments.)

10. What is your appointment policy? Can we just walk in if our child is sick?

It's always best to start searching for a pediatrician early in the second trimester. That way you have plenty of time to look around — and you might need plenty of time. After all, you're looking for a doctor who will take care of your child for the next 18 years, so you've got every right to be picky.

The Well-Child Visit

You might not know this, but babies have a set schedule for when they need to go see the pediatrician. They're called well-child visits, and basically they're there for you to take the little ankle biter in and get him seen by the doctor. She will look him over and make sure he's growing like he should, maturing in certain specific ways, looking healthy, getting enough to eat, and receiving all his scheduled vaccinations.

No little dude or dudette will like going to most of these well-child visits, but it's something that has to be done. Just get ready to suffer through the screaming. And you might even be able to hear your child yell over the sound of all your whimpering.

The first time you'll take your little dudette in to see the doctor will be when she's a week or two old. It's likely that you'll have lots of questions that will come from trying to take care of a baby in the wild. We're sure you'll be a little intimidated by all the stuff you're trying to learn (it's why we're here, after all), so it's probably a good idea to write these down before you go into the office. The hard part is actually remembering to bring them with you when you leave the house. Our advice? Put your list of questions in the diaper bag. You're not going out of the house without that, so the list should make it with you.

After the initial well-child visit, you should bring your little

10 questions every dude should ask the doc

1. Is this normal? (This is the time to ask about any problem you're not sure about. Seriously, ask *anything*. Doctors went to years more school than you did, so they're pretty sure to know a bit more about your baby's anatomy than you do. It's okay for you not to know everything.)

2. Was this supposed to fall off? (No, seriously. For instance, your little dudette will have a bit of the umbilical cord still attached to her navel. Eventually, it will dry up and fall off. It can be a bit shocking if you don't know about it beforehand.)

3. Is there someone specific in your office I should call if I have a health question about my son?

4. My wife/partner is having a hard time getting our daughter to breast/bottle-feed. Do you have any hints, or is there anyone to talk to about this? (There are lactation specialists, many of whom work for doctors or hospitals, who know all about breast-feeding.)

5. Do these jeans make my butt look fat?

6. I'm *pretty sure* our car seat is buckled in correctly, but how can I find out for sure?

7. Shouldn't my son be (crawling/smiling/laughing/grasping/ juggling) by now? (It's tempting to see developmental milestones as goals to meet, but don't. They're just general guidelines for when some children start doing specific things. If your child is early, that doesn't mean he's a genius. Likewise, if he's a little late, that doesn't mean you should go into mourning.)

8. Can I have my child's upcoming vaccination schedule, and can you explain what each shot is designed to protect against? (If you have any questions about vaccinations, this is the time to ask. Make sure you understand that these vaccinations are very necessary and safe.)

9. When should I start to consider solid foods? For the baby, I mean, not me.

10. When should she start sleeping through the night? (Most developmental milestones will be covered by the doc, but we figure #9 and #10 are the two that are going to be driving you nuts, and if that's the case, feel free to ask about them again. Just to be sure.)

dudette in for follow-up visits when she's two, four, six, nine, 12, 15, 18, and 24 months old. After that, doctors usually want to see your child once a year for regular checkups. We've found it's best to schedule those visits around your little dudette's birthday. That way, it's easier to remember that she's due for an appointment.

Sometimes, of course, you're going to need to make unexpected visits to the pediatrician. There's nothing that makes you feel as helpless as watching your little dudette get sick. Your heart breaks as you see her cry and yell and grab at something on her body that hurts. Or watch her defeated body language after she's just thrown up.

It's horrible.

Feeling helpless when one's child is in pain is something no one wants to face, but it's going to be a fact of life. Even after you've taken your little dudette to the doctor, gotten her prescription filled, and done everything you can, the desire to *do* something more to help is going to be nearly overpowering.

So we came up with a great idea.

Fake it.

Apparently, we're not the first ones to think this thing through. An older friend of ours (older than us, that is; we're not going to call *him* old because he'd probably kick both of our butts) said that on occasion, doing something that's not medically helpful can work wonders when it's done with love.

Ed: *I hated that feeling of helplessness. And I think it* *was even worse for me since I'm a doctor. My whole job revolves around looking at people in pain and finding ways to help them, then actually doing something about it.*

After I'd done everything I could medically do to make sure my young daughter was getting the best care, I still felt like I had to do something.

What I would do is hold her, not too close if she had a fever since I didn't want her to get too hot. But I'd hold her and then gently apply a cool, wet washcloth to the back of her neck and to her forehead.

I know it didn't have all that much — if any — medicinal value, but I think it made her feel better, and I know it made me feel better.

It was something my mother would do for me when I was a little kid, and I still remember that feeling of cool cutting through the fever, knowing my mom was there for me, loving me and doing all she could for me.

I wanted my daughter to get that same feeling. So, every time she was sick as a baby, I'd do the same thing. I'd softly wipe sweat from her forehead and gently rest the cool washcloth on her neck. It really seemed to take some of her pain away.

Now, we're obviously not telling you that, if your little dude is sick, the best or only thing you can do is to put a wet washcloth on his head. That would be silly. But being there for him is not.

We've already touched on how you should go about trying

to secure a pediatrician for your little dude. Now let's talk a little about when you should go to see her — and when you should speak first to her nurse.

For example, what are you supposed to do if your child is feeling out of sorts, and there's no well-child visit scheduled?

Well, the first thing you need to do is to make a note of his symptoms. Sometimes it's as vague as just *knowing* he's not acting right. Often, though, you can see he might be tired, or has a fever, or is throwing up, or has diarrhea. You'll want to keep some means of taking a temperature in the house. There are several different methods out there, but we'll leave that to you to choose, since you'll know which one you feel most comfortable with.

When your little dude isn't feeling well and it's more than that he's just cranky, you should not pack him up and head for the doctor's office right away. The best thing for you to do is to call the doctor's office and ask to speak to the triage nurse. The triage nurse will listen to your list of symptoms and make a very loose, very tentative diagnosis. What you tell her will help her decide whether you should bring your little dude in to see the doctor or not. Make sure you give the nurse a good listen. There's going to be some really good advice coming to you, so have a pen and some paper close by when you make the call.

After that, it's just a question of following directions and hoping you can make it through your little dude's sickness without getting it yourself.

Richard: *My mom used to ask, "What good is an*

immune system if you don't challenge it every once in a while?"

By that, she meant that she would never try especially hard to keep away from my sister or me when we were sick. Either her immune system would rout the disease, or she'd get it and then add it to the arsenal of diseases her immune system could defeat.

That, in itself, wouldn't be too bad if it weren't for her other way of boosting her immune system. And ours. She always thought the five-second rule was much too strict. If some food dropped to the floor, she saw no reason it couldn't go into our little baby mouths after a few minutes, whether or not it has been squashed underfoot.

My sons have no idea how good they have it. I mean, for years, when I was growing up, I thought Twinkies came out of the box already squished flat.

5

making the cut?

yes, we're talkin' 'bout circumcision

Keep calm. Don't panic. It's only a word.

Okay, now that you've resumed breathing, let's talk.

Little dudes are born with what is called foreskin, a layer of skin that covers the head, or glans, of the penis. The foreskin on newborns, unlike that on older boys, can't be pushed back at all. However, if the little dude gets circumcised, then the foreskin is cut away, leaving the head visible.

If you decide not to get your son circumcised, then over the next few years the foreskin will gradually separate from the head of the penis and can be pushed back.

So, if the same results will be achieved over time, why put the baby (and his parents) through the ordeal of getting this little bit of skin cut off his penis?

Well, if you're Jewish or Islamic, getting your infant son circumcised is a symbol of his covenant with God or Allah. In the Jewish religion, infant boys are circumcised eight days after they are born. In the Muslim faith, the ritual is often performed when the male baby is seven days old, but it can be later, within the first few years of the child's life. In both of these religions, it's an important tradition, although calling it a tradition might be underselling its sacred significance and deep-rooted meaning. What we're trying to say is that there's a reason it's been going on for a reeeallly long time. In fact, circumcision is thought to be the oldest medical procedure still performed today.

In the United States, it's become general medical practice for most little dudes to get circumcised in the first few days after they are born. This trend really got started in the late 1800s, and it's been going strong ever since.

There have been a number of justifications for the routine circumcision of baby boys. Among them is that it makes the head of the penis less sensitive (it doesn't), which would, therefore, make masturbation less tempting. Another early justification was that circumcision would cure epilepsy, syphilis, asthma, lunacy, and TB. Medical science has since discounted all of these claims. Opponents of circumcision argue that not even well-meaning parents have the right to choose for this procedure to be performed on an infant who is obviously way too young to give his consent.

In a position paper issued in 2012, the American Academy of Pediatrics reversed its long-standing neutrality on circumcision. According to the new policy, the health benefits of having a baby boy circumcised outweigh the risks. Some of the research that led to this new stance came from studies that took place in Africa, which suggest that the procedure might help protect heterosexual men against infection by HIV. The organization stopped short of recommending that all baby boys be circumcised. The decision to circumcise, the Academy policy reads, should remain a family decision.

Regardless of any official policy, circumcision has marched

merrily along and continues to be done in most hospitals. A lot of the time, little dudes get circumcised because their big dudes were circumcised. The thinking goes that you wouldn't want the little dude to look at you and then look at himself and wonder why you look different from each other. In our culture, sex (and anything related to it) is a sensitive subject that can unfairly cause a lot of angst. Thinking you're strange because your penis looks different can stir up a number of insecurities and sensitivities.

However, according to some statistics we read in a book (so you wouldn't have to), the percentage of circumcisions done each year in the United States has been going down since the 1990s, dropping from 62.7 percent in 1999 to only 54.5 percent in 2009.

So, bottom line: do your homework, and make an educated decision on how you and your partner want to proceed.

If you both have decided to have the little dude circumcised, it will probably be done early on at the hospital. After the procedure is completed, the doctor will apply some petroleum jelly and a temporary bandage to your infant son's penis. The bandage will come off the next time the little dude pees.

The most important thing you need to do is to keep his penis as clean as possible until it is completely healed. Then, of course, you just keep it really, really clean until he's able to take over the job. Make sure when you are cleaning the little dude's circumcised penis that you are as gentle as possible. (Remember, no matter how routine you think it might be, it's still surgery and it's going to hurt.) Use mild soap and water to clean it.

Washing a circumcised penis following the operation is a tricky bit of business. See, the skin where the shaft meets the glans is going to be healing from the removal of the foreskin. Healing skin doesn't really discriminate much, which means that if skin is touching healing skin, it's going to heal together. You don't want that to happen in this case because then, when the penis becomes erect, the healed-together shaft and glans skin will not allow the penis to find its full extension.

With that in mind, you need to get a Q-tip and some antibiotic ointment. Put some of the ointment on the Q-tip and set it aside so nothing gets on the ointment. Gently but firmly pull the skin from the shaft down toward your infant son's body, exposing the site of the circumcision. Make sure there is no skin stuck anywhere. When the site of the circumcision is exposed, carefully wipe it with the antibiotic ointment. Not only will this help protect it against infection, but the lubricating agent in the ointment will help prevent the skin from healing the wrong way.

In the days, weeks, and years to come, you'll need to continue doing this on a semi-regular basis when he's getting a bath. Even when the circumcision is healed, skin can still stick to itself if left in contact with more skin in a damp, dark place. You don't want him to get a diaper rash on his penis, so make sure to keep it clean.

After the circumcision, the penis will look very red, and there might be a yellowish secretion coming from the tip. Don't worry. Both are indications that the penis is healing naturally. But if the redness and secretion don't start to go away by the end of the first week following the procedure, it may be that your little dude has some kind of infection. If that happens, you should take him to see his pediatrician.

If you decide not to circumcise, you're not totally off the hook. There's still some stuff you need to know about how to care for the little dude's penis. All you need to do during the first few months is to wash it with mild soap and water. Because the foreskin is connected to the head of the penis, it won't roll back, so don't try. Also, don't try cleaning the opening in the foreskin with a Q-tip. As long as you're cleaning it with soap and water in a regular bath, the uncircumcised penis should be just fine.

After several months or years, the foreskin will separate from the head of the penis and can then be retracted. Once that is possible, you'll need to retract the foreskin occasionally during baths to clean the penis underneath.

We realize we've probably told you more than you ever thought you'd need to know about circumcision, but we believe it's important for you big dudes to know how to take care of your little dudes. Whether you decide to circumcise or not is a choice that's up to you and your partner. We're just here to give you the facts, man . . . er, dude. We'll talk more about keeping the penis clean in the section on bathing. We bet you can't wait for that!

6

hold him like
a football,
but
be careful not
to spike him

low weight, high reps

• •

You're about to embark on a great exercise program, an athletic adventure like no other. All those years of Little League and pee wee football are about to pay off handsomely. Now that you've got a little dude, you're going to be doing a lot of weight lifting. You're going to be climbing stairs with weights. You'll be walking with weights. You'll be balancing with weights. And, oddly enough, all the weights will weigh exactly the same as your little dude.

However, you can't just hold him any old way. There are any number of ways to hold him, and many of those ways are very, very wrong. There are also a few ways that are right, and we'll tell you about some of them here. Of course, there will be other ways that we don't cover, but we suggest that you ask your pediatrician if you have any questions about holding your little dude.

> **Barry:** *My favorite method of holding is the Heisman cradle. What I do is to rest her head just below my armpit and on my bicep. (That means I have to keep clean and smelling good. Not that much of a problem.) Then her body rests along my arm. Her butt rests in the crook of my elbow and her legs are balanced on my forearm and near my hand. That way I can get her resting against my body and have a good, firm grip on*

her outside, upper thigh. I can fend off dangers, or stiff-arm tacklers, with my right hand and, with my left, I've got a great hold on my daughter's leg. That way, if she slips and I have to grab her, I won't hurt her. If I slip, I can use my right hand to catch myself.

There are a number of reasons why you never want to support all of her weight just by holding onto her arm, but the prime one is that her arm is relatively delicate and can break or dislocate much more easily than her leg. Of course, if she's falling and the only way to stop that is to grab her arm, go for it. Better to grab her arm than for her to fall on her head.

You'll also need to learn how to pick up newborn babies. When your little dude is born, he's going to have very, very weak neck muscles. That means he won't be able to hold his head up well at all. So, when you do pick him up, you need to use as safe a technique as possible. The way we were taught is to put your hands under his back, with your thumbs through each armpit. Then your fingers will be in place to support his head as you lift.

Richard: *One way I liked to hold each of my little dudes when they were babies was to pick them up using the method described above. For example, I'd hold Sarcasmo to my chest, with his face going either to the right or the left, and his legs dangling down. I'd have one hand under his butt and one hand holding his head to my chest. That way I could smell his head and kiss the holes in the top of his head. Yeah, I'm a big softy. Wanna make somethin' of it?*

There's a Hole in His Head!

Yeah, we might want to back up a little bit here. At the end of the previous page, Richard really did talk about gently kissing the holes in the top of his little dude's head. And he made it sound so normal. Oddly, that's not only because he thinks of the oddest things as being normal, but also because it really *is* normal for newborn little dudes to have actual holes in their skulls.

What we mean is that, by the time your baby is born, his skull still won't be fully formed. He will have two soft spots, also called fontanels. Don't worry about it. Your baby isn't unique, at least not in *that* way. *All* babies have soft spots when they're born, when the only thing protecting their brains is a thick membrane under their oh-so-soft skin and hair. In other words, not all that much. These fontanels, or soft spots, are the places where the little dude's immature skull bones have not quite grown together. The good news is that these holes are only temporary. They will grow together.

The soft spots are located in two places. The first and largest is on the top of his head toward the front. The second, smaller soft spot is at the back. And while the fontanels will feel strange, you shouldn't be afraid to touch them, as long as you do so gently.

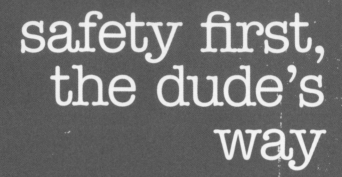

safety first, the dude's way

do you know the way to Lowe's?

We listened to our moms. We heard her tell us all the time that the world was a dangerous place and that the only way to stay safe was to listen to her words of wisdom and do exactly what she said. Now, we're not saying that we did that *all* the time, but we're still alive, so that means we, and she, must have done something right.

Which brings us to our next point: safety.

When you first bring your baby home, she's not going to be doing much aside from lying there, sleeping, peeing, pooping, and screaming. Sure, it's a full schedule, but there's not much room in there for getting around the house and into trouble.

> **Richard:** *Actually, that was one of my favorite times with my boys. When they're that little, you can set them down in the middle of the floor, and if you have to run an errand in the house, you can do it. And, even better, when you get back, the baby will still be in the exact same place. But you can't get lulled into laziness here. You've always got to watch your little dude and check on him.*

That sense of peace will change as soon as she starts to crawl. When she gets mobile, everything is fair game. That lovely vase on the table? Shattered on the kitchen floor. All those neat-looking bottles of stuff with the skulls on them under the sink? She wonders if they taste as good as they look. Those enamel football helmets you just got from eBay? Missing, probably for good.

So, yeah, it's definitely a good idea to get cracking on making sure your house is baby safe. Now, that doesn't necessarily mean that you have to cover everything in foam, place a fingerprint-recognition lock on every door, and brick up every stairway, but you *do* have some work to do.

Before you get busy watching the little dude and baby-proofing the kitchen, remember: the problem with multitasking is that babies can't be multitasked. They demand 100 percent of your attention, and not just because they're selfish and self-centered. Although they are.

When you're with your infant dudette, every sense you've got (plus a few you'll develop as you become used to being a dad, which we'll get into in another chapter) has to be focused on the tiny, helpless bundle of poop and smiles in your arms. Smell for any deposits that need to be cleaned out. Feel for the first signs of a fever. Watch to see any behavior that deviates from the norm and needs to be investigated. Listen for that especially bloodcurdling scream that indicates a titanic gassy bubble just waiting to be coaxed out of one end or the other. Taste your own desperation when you realize you *could* get the score on your phone, but that would be another task added to the one you are already doing, and that's a no-no.

Taking care of a little dude is like driving, only without the sense of knowing where you're going or the ability to control how you get there.

When you drive, you're not supposed to be texting or talking on the phone or watching a movie or writing a love note to your wife (as dudes often do). To be safe, you need to give 100 percent of your attention to the task of driving. Even if you are going a bit too fast or too slow, it's more than likely going to be all right, because all those other drivers are — hopefully — giving their total attention to what's going on as well.

Little dudes, however, do not give any percent of their attention to their own health and welfare. Mostly, they just scream, sleep, or poop. You're the one who has to come in after and comfort, tuck, or clean and make it all better. Because if you're not there to watch out for your little dude, he's certainly not going to do it for himself. He can't.

No pressure there, right?

We're going to give you a big break and assume that nothing catastrophic is going to happen with your little dude or little dudette. (You're welcome.) Still, there's a lot of territory to cover between perfect health and happiness, and catastrophe. You can do a lot to keep it closer to the healthy and happy end of the continuum by giving up multitasking and focusing all of your attention — that's *every single drop you have* — on your little dude when you're with him.

Don't think of it as a punishment, but as a requirement. After all, you did get to have the fun of creation. So, now it's time to see what you've wrought. Besides, they're sooooo cuuuuute. She's bound to do something more wonderfuler than any other baby ever. That's her job.

Now go do yours.

And by that we mean, of course, it's time to make some changes to your house. It's time to do some renovation with safety in mind. We're talking her safety, dudes. We assume that you won't saw off any of your own important body parts. . . .

The following section is about things you'll need for babyproofing your house. It's not all-inclusive, but that's because we don't know what your house looks like. (At least as far as you know.) You'll have to take these basics and then apply some critical thinking to the rest of your house. We know, thinking hurts, but it will be worth it.

Get Smart, Get Safe

Making your home safe is more than filling in the ticky boxes on a checklist, it's an attitude. Sure, some people might call that attitude paranoia, but we like to think of it as a realistic appraisal of potential dangers. We don't think the world is out to get us, and neither should you. (Although it is.) No, what you need to do is to think like a little dude: view the world around you as a marvelous place full of cool stuff, and you want to see all of it. And then put it in your mouth.

You might have noticed, your little dude is not as tall as you. What you might not have considered is that this difference in elevation leads to a significantly different outlook on things. Stuff you don't see because you're towering over the scene might be at perfect eye level for your easily distracted and even-more-easily tempted little dude.

Which means it's playtime. Get down on the floor with your little dude and look at things from his perspective. Get the lowdown on the situation by crawling around your house. Stop everywhere you see something you might need to change, make a note of it, and then keep crawling.

Be on the lookout for wires he can pull or put into his mouth, tight spaces in which he can get stuck, access to dangerous places, sharp corners where he can bump his head, breakable stuff, things that are small enough to fit into his mouth (because if they can fit into his mouth, they *will* go into his mouth), places where he can make a summiting attempt and pull down something on top of himself in the process — look for all of these things and more.

The first thing you need to throw out (no, it's not your dignity — that's long gone) is any preconception you may have about what he would — or wouldn't — do. You might think, "There's no way he'd do that. No one's that dumb." Guess what? He is *that* dumb. Because he's had no experience at doing anything. He has no past history to draw on. He's got nothing to guide him in making a decision. All he's got is what's right in front of him. And what's right in front of him is shiny and cool and looks tasty.

Starting to get the picture?

Manly Men and the Manliness They Make

Over tens of thousands of years, we came down out of the trees, moved away from the savannah, and began grouping together to form nations and cultures. Whether this was a good idea or not is still up for debate. What we know is that our roles as men and as parents have changed significantly. We no longer *have* to go out and hunt for our food, or plow the ground to raise crops, or build our own homes. Which means our skill sets have changed drastically over the last few decades.

Not many dudes know how to inspect the carburetor in their cars or change the oil, or knock out a wall to put in a window, or build a bookcase. For most dudes, that little toolbox gathering dust out there in the garage has a hammer for putting nails into the wall on which to hang pictures, and a couple of screwdrivers to pry open the backs of remotes to put in new batteries.

And that's . . . okay.

We understand that not everyone is a handyman. Think of it this way: not many handymen can do what you do. So we're even.

However, there's a certain macho manliness that accrues to the dude who can do some of the physical work around the house — maybe put in a ceiling fan, or get the garbage disposal working right. Achieving that can make you walk around with your chest puffed out and a superior smirk on your face for days. So, now we're going to give you some jobs to do. Not only will you be doing manly man work, you'll also be making the house safe for your little dude.

Here's the deal. After you do your crawl-around-the-house reconnaissance mission, draw up a list of the trouble spots you've found.

Now you're set.

It's time to hit that most manliest of manly places: Lowe's hardware superstore. Aisles and aisles of wood and power tools and manual tools and pipes and locks and hinges and doors and . . . and . . . We think you get the point.

The good news is that Lowe's, Home Depot, and other stores of a similar ilk have everything you're going to need to get the job done. The better news is that you don't even have to know all that much to be able to babyproof your home by yourself. As long as you can use a screwdriver or powered screwdriver, you're in.

So you hit Lowe's with a list, strutting down the aisle, filling up the cart. Yeah, that's right, you're making the world safe for your little dude. You're protecting your family. Nothing manlier than that.

We know that some of you get a bit nervous stalking the aisles of Lowe's because there's so much stuff there and you have no idea what most of it does, but this is one time you don't have to worry. So relax. Most of the stuff you buy to babyproof your house will have easy-to-follow directions and is simple to figure out once you look at it.

In case you need help, we've put together some basic items that should probably be on everybody's list. As we said, this isn't a comprehensive selection, and not everything on it will be available at Lowe's, but it's a good place to start. Remember to do your own research before setting out to the store. Another good idea is to talk to the helpful employees there and ask if they have any ideas. We'll bet you'll find a few dads and moms among them.

1. **Corner guards.** These indispensable foam doohickeys are great. You simply slip them over corners, like, say, the very sharp edge of your coffee table on which you've already bruised your shin a couple of times. Babies, once they're mobile, love to move around. When they can stand, it's even worse. Because they'll pull up on anything and then start wobbling around. And then they'll fall. Everywhere. Having a sharp corner in that danger zone is just asking for trouble. Babies tend to crawl and walk without any regard to their own safety or even attention to where they're going. They just want to move. These corner guards aren't decorative. They won't make the room look better, but they will make it safer.

2. **Cabinet locks.** These are plastic doohickeys that come in two parts. There's a part that attaches to the inside frame of the cabinet and a part that attaches to the door of the cabinet. When you close the door, these two parts interlock and hold together, preventing the door from opening. Well, they do that unless an adult, or someone with significantly better motor coordination than a baby, pinches or prods or pokes the lock in the correct fashion.

   Cabinet locks are great, and they do a lot of good. However, we must caution that they're not perfect. They *can* open up for a baby. In which case, it would be a good thing if there weren't any potentially toxic chemicals or cleaning supplies readily available for the little dude to get into. Move these items to a different location for a while, out of the reach of tiny, curious hands.

3. **Drawer locks.** These can be found in the same area of the store as the cabinet locks, and they follow a similar principle. You want to make sure that you lock the drawers, especially if they're stacked one on top of the other. These locks prevent the baby from getting into the drawers and from using them as a ladder to climb even higher.

4. **Doorknob covers.** You probably won't need these for the first year or so — at least until the little dudette can stand up by herself — but buy a set of them for all your doors just to be ready for when you'll need them. They are plastic and snap loosely over your doorknobs. Little hands are too small to squeeze them and turn the knob, but big hands can do it easily. It stops the little dudette from getting out to wander the neighborhood by herself. If you've got levers for door handles, there are covers for them as well. Also, grab a couple of toilet straps and fridge straps. These will keep the toilet cover securely closed, and the same thing for the fridge doors.

5. **Changing pads.** Make sure you have a couple of different changing pads, waterproofed and fully lined, that you can rest your baby on to change the diaper. Have a few strategically located near the floor in different rooms. When you've got a stinky, crying baby, you don't want to have to go running from room to room looking for a changing pad to put on the floor. We recommend changing your little dudette on the floor rather than on a table or other high surface from which she can take a nasty fall. The pad should have a safety belt with a plastic buckle that will keep your little dudette safely on the pad so she doesn't roll across the floor. Make sure

that once she's belted in it's not possible for her to tumble over and pull the pad on top of her. Think ahead to avoid worst-case scenarios.

Some parents prefer a central location to change their baby's diaper, but when Richard's little dudes were still floor scrubbers, he had diaper-changing stations throughout the house. He carried supplies for each station in a small purple shower caddy, which contained everything he needed to change his little dudes.

6. **Faucet covers.** Not only do they come in a bunch of cool shapes for little babies, like fish and whales and stuff, they also provide a nice cushion to keep your little dude from whacking his face into the hard metal faucet.

7. **Expandable safety gates and fences.** Make sure you get one made from sturdy plastic all the way through, with only small or no openings in the bars or the mesh. You don't want to get the kind that has large openings your little dudette can put her head, arms, or feet through. Pressure-mounted gates do a great job of keeping babies off stairs and out of dangerous rooms. You simply adjust them until they fit, and then expand them a bit more so they stay in place. It's so simple, even *we* could set them up. Also, you might want to investigate the sorts of hardware-mounted safety gates that are bolted directly into the wall. Provided you put them up correctly, and you will, you manly dude, you will, they could be even more stable than the pressure-mounted gates.

8. **Outlet covers.** These come in a variety of different shapes and are a great idea. You're going to have electrical outlets all over the place. You're also going to

have a inquisitive little dudette who doesn't know she shouldn't stick a finger or anything else in there. There are barrier covers, which prevent anything from going in. There also are covers you can mount in place of the previous frame, which can flip open or slide back, allowing better access to the electrical outlet. Whichever style you choose, you need to pick up a bunch.

9. **Baby monitor.** You can probably find this in a wide range of different places, including most online stores, and you will probably be overwhelmed by the sheer number and variety of monitors. Don't worry. As long as your monitor allows you to clearly hear what's going on in the baby's room, you're all good. There are some with features that allow you to talk to the baby, and others that combine a speaking monitor with CCTV so you can watch what's happening as well. Just make sure that you fully understand how to work the model you buy. When a dude has a baby, he's allowed to ask as many questions as he wants.

10. **Door stops.** You don't have to use your phone book or dictionary as a door stop anymore. The ones we're talking about are affixed to the tops of doors and prevent them from closing all the way without some adult intervention. We'd recommend that you put these on the bathroom doors and on the baby bedroom door. You do not want to have your little dudette crawl into the bathroom and close the door, only to find that someone had pushed the lock earlier and now precious is locked in there. These also will prevent doors from slamming shut on tiny, trusting fingers.

pop's quiz

can you be too safe?

1 **When you went to the store(s) to buy stuff so you could babyproof your two-bedroom apartment, how did you carry the purchases out of the store?**
   A. in a few plastic sacks
   B. in the shopping cart
   C. Carry? You backed up your friend's moving van.

2 **When you take your little dude out for a walk in the park, do you . . .**
   A. make sure to bring the stroller, diaper bag, and a change of clothes?
   B. put him in his Class-A environmental suit, hook up the oxygen supply, and tell the bodyguards to clear a 30-meter security cordon around the park?
   C. ask who's going outside? Just turn on the virtual simulator's spring-breeze feature, because he sure as heck isn't going out there!

3 **You see a babyproofed cabinet door in the kitchen that is hanging open because the plastic latch has broken. Now, while your little dudette is napping, what do you do?**
   A. Make sure she's still asleep, and then get the tools you'll need from the garage.
   B. Barricade her bedroom door closed to make sure your daughter can't hop the crib fence, wriggle down the hall, and get into the stuff in the cabinet. You then grab the handy duct tape and start running strips of the tape across the entire front of the cabinet. Just to be sure.
   C. Throw yourself at the cabinet, hanging on by the sink. Use your body to completely cover the loose door, because you don't want her to see it and get curious. After an hour of hanging on your side, you wonder if you might need to seek professional help. Decide against it and get a better grip. On the sink.

If you answered A to the preceding questions, you've probably got a good handle on the difference between protection and freezing your little dude in carbonite to keep him safe. If you answered B to any or all of the above, you're beginning to look at carbonite as the wimp's way out of child protection. If you answered C to any of the questions, we need to have a very long, very serious talk. We'll bring the tranquilizers.

The Not-So-Secret Six

Even before your little dude comes home from the hospital, you should already be thinking about ways to make your house safer for his soon-to-be-everywhere-yes-even-there hands. Making your home a testament to the art of baby-proofing will show off your very manly prowess with power tools and installing, but it's also going to take a considerable amount of time and money to do. As soon as you think you're done, up pops something else that needs work. That's life. Especially one with a new little dude in it.

However, because we like you so much, we're going to give you some quick tips on places to start making your home a monument to the padded-room school of home decorating. Minus the long-sleeved white jackets that button up the back.

Here, with no further ado (and very little to do as well) are the six things you can do right now, for free, to make your home safer for the new little dude.

1) Move the changing spot. Seriously, no matter how cute that changing pad on top of the dresser looked to your wife in the store, there's no disputing the fact that it's still four feet up in the air, and so's the little dudette. Start changing her on the ground, or, at least, closer to it.

2) Make sure your blinds are as safe as they are chic. Even if they're not the least bit chic, you still should make them safe. Start with those pesky cords that open and shut — as well as raise and lower — the blinds. These cords, and we can't stress this enough, can be lethal to a small baby. Tie them up, far, far out of harm's way.

3) Go in the bathroom and take a good look around: if anything is plugged in, move it far away from the bath or the sink you'll be using to bathe the little dude. As you know, electricity and water certainly don't mix. They mix even less well when there's a little dude around, flailing his cute, grabby arms and high-kicking legs all over the place.

4) Turn down the temperature on your water heater. Unlike our coarse, grown-up skin, baby skin is soft and tender — and that means it can burn a lot easier. Adjust the water temperature to no more than 110 degrees. That's still plenty hot for you, but won't scald the little dude.

5) Plan for the future, and do a little *feng shui*. Rearrange your rooms so that you don't have any climbable furniture under your windows. Open windows make it easier for a climbing baby to head out. While we're at it, you might want to put a screw into each window frame, about six inches or so above the window. That way, the window can't go up any higher. Unless your baby is somehow related to Plastic Man or Mr. Fantastic, we're pretty sure she's not getting out that window.

6) Finally, haul out your phone and your wife's phone as well, and put the numbers for your pediatrician, poison control, and the hospital ER into speed dial. Also, post those numbers in a central, easily accessible place in your home. If anything happens, you don't want to be searching for the right number to call.

Even if you didn't join the Boy Scouts, it's still a great idea to follow their motto: Be prepared. Now, you've got a few simple tasks to start you off on the right path. Once you're done, it'll be that much easier to move on to the next steps on your babyproofing agenda.

One of the most important rooms you'll need to cross off your to-do list is the kitchen. Babies and kitchens go together like onions and ice cream, like the Louvre and crushed-velvet paintings of John Wayne, like a sweaty body and grass clippings. It's not a good idea, is what we're saying. So much can go wrong there, so quickly and devastatingly. We're not advocating exiling your little dude or dudette from the kitchen permanently, but just be aware of all the dangers that lurk there.

Here's a short list: knives, forks, electrical outlets, falling drawers, swinging cabinets, knives, falling fridge shelves, fire, boiling stuff, fire, and knives.

So, yeah, there's a lot that can go wrong.

> **Richard:** *Just around the time my sister, Tia, learned to walk, she was in the kitchen with our mom, who was frying something at the stove.*
>
> *You can already see where this is going. Yeah, Tia managed to stretch just enough to disturb the pan handle. The pan tumbled and hit Tia, splashing the frying oil on her.*
>
> *Fortunately, she wasn't scalded too badly and the burns gradually healed, but it was a scary and horrible time there for a while. To this day, and there were many days in between, Tia will not fry anything in her kitchen. Even*

as an adult she's nervous about frying oil because of that experience.

Not everyone can be as lucky as Tia and escape permanent physical injury. Barry has a friend who has scars all over her body from getting burned as a baby in the kitchen. It can happen to anyone.

Kitchens: Full of peril, and that's before we even add your cooking into the equation. Just kidding. About your cooking. Not the danger.

Cooking is a tough situation when you've got a little dude in the room. If you can't keep him out of the kitchen (and even if you think you have), make sure that all pot and pan handles are pointing away from the front of the stove. Try to cook on the back burner as much as possible. This will make it almost impossible for the little dude to get up there and tip something hot over on himself, or get scorched by the flames of the gas burner. (Unless someone left the drawers unlatched and he manages to crawl up there on his own.)

One important piece of safety equipment a lot of people forget to use is a cover for the burner on a stove. Whether you have electric or gas burners, you need to have something that will cover up the hot points. That way, even if the little dude manages to turn the knobs controlling the heat, there still won't be a naked heat source ready to burn little fingers.

The first thing you need to consider is getting a baby gate to put in the doorway of the kitchen. As we mentioned earlier, a baby gate is an expandable fence that keeps babies out of potential danger zones. Having a baby gate across a doorway to the kitchen can be a nuisance for you to navigate, but it'll be impossible for your little dude to get into the kitchen without you knowing it — and that's worth the extra work on your part.

Every single drawer in your kitchen needs to have a latch on it to prevent it from opening unless an adult does the fiddling. It's going to be a pain in the butt for you to open a drawer in your kitchen after this, but it will prevent your little dude from pulling it down on his head or tugging it open and finding the knives when you've momentarily glanced at the TV to see Cam Newton throw the winning touchdown.

In addition to the latches on the drawers, make sure you install secure latches on your refrigerator and cabinets, especially those that contain cleaning supplies or other chemicals. There are several different styles of cabinet latches, but we prefer the one that requires you to stick your hand into the partially open cabinet drawer and pinch shut a plastic safety catch. That definitely requires some dexterity that little dudes just can't pull off.

The biggest safety installation in the kitchen, though, isn't something you can buy. It's *you*. Your brain always has to be on alert, not on automatic pilot. When your little dude is in the kitchen, you must be aware of what's going on in the moment and what could happen in the future. Our money's on the guy who said "'Safety First' is 'Safety Always.'"

The Baby in Your Head

One of the most important things we want you to take away from this book is the holy trinity (if we can be forgiven for using a religious simile in a nonreligious context): keep your little dude safe, fed and sheltered (which we're counting as one), and clean. That's the foundation on which everything else depends.

Safety can encompass so many things that it's probably the biggest category. You need to be concerned about the environment in which the baby lives: Is there lead in the paint? Are there choking hazards? Sharp corners? Is the changing table too high? Is the car seat attached correctly? Do I have enough clothing and sunblock to protect her when we go outside?

It can be overwhelming, no question about it. To make matters worse, even when you think you've covered everything, when you believe you're doing every single thing right, you can still get tricked by time.

Take, for example, our friend Carter. He and his wife had been raising their firstborn son and doing a great job of it. The only time their son saw the inside of a doctor's office was on well-child visits. No boo-boos of any sort. He was a happy kid.

The little dude had also recently learned to crawl. And he'd taken to it like a pig in slop, or a dude to a couch. He was crawling everywhere. Any time he could get onto the ground, he was scooting off to explore somewhere new. Since this independent streak had just begun to emerge, Carter wasn't yet aware of how far and wide his son could travel.

Because he's the type of dude he is, Carter volunteered to get up with his son early (and this being a baby, we're talking crack-of-dawn early) on a Saturday morning. Carter did everything right. He went to get his son, smiled happily at the loud little dude, and got him changed and fed in no time.

> **Carter:** *Feeding him was something I really loved. It was such fun to hold his little body in my arms and give him the bottle. His face showed such pure bliss, like he was really enjoying the simple things. And I enjoyed him.*
>
> *Once I'd finished getting him fed, burped, and changed, I held him in my lap for a little bit and just made goofy faces at him for a while. He was a baby. That's what they think is fun. We played for a while and I managed to tire him out. Since we were already on the floor and he was passed out, I just covered him with his favorite wubby (which, in nonparent-speak, is a blanket) and gave him a toy.*
>
> *I was drifting off to sleep myself when I suddenly sat up. That's when I remembered that I'd left my breakfast warming up in the oven. I didn't want it to brown to a crisp, especially since it was something I was cooking for my wife as well. I had plans for winning a lot of husband points that morning.*
>
> *I wasn't really thinking, you know. I didn't consider anything new that had happened in the past week. I didn't think. My son was asleep on the floor, perfectly safe, right?*
>
> *I was downstairs, setting the breakfast down to cool when I heard this horrible thumping noise. I knew exactly what it was. Even now I hear that sound sometimes and I still get that awful dropping sensation in my stomach. I*

dropped the breakfast and sprinted out of the kitchen.

He hadn't even begun to cry, but you could see it coming. My son lay on the floor, his little hands balled into fists and his legs shooting out straight, every muscle clenched. He opened his mouth and screamed. Loud. So loud he woke my wife up quickly.

Well, to make a long story short, he wasn't hurt beyond a couple of bruises. I think I got more bruises than he did, but, then again, my wife has better aim than the stairs. It was just horrible. I can't tell you how guilty I felt, how low, how terrible.

I'd thought the house was safe. My son never really moved around in the past, you know? That's what I was thinking. His crawling thing was so new. It just never even occurred to me that he might wake up and get out of the room. He'd changed and I hadn't kept up.

Thank goodness, though, that he turned out to be all right once he calmed down. I swear, though, I think he glared at me for weeks after.

Carter got lucky, and he knew it. The thing is that while he should have taken elementary safety precautions like putting up the baby fence they'd purchased for the stairs as soon as his child began crawling, we understand how this all-too-human mistake could happen: the baby in his head was sedentary. He just assumed the baby-in-the-real-world would stay where he'd been set down. The baby in Carter's head hadn't caught up with the baby in his life.

All of which illustrates an important lesson of being a dad:

you've got to be on your toes, alert every second you're around your child. It's not easy, but no one ever said being a dad would be. Well, except for teenaged kids who think they know everything, but that's another problem for another day.

Even when everything is right in the little dudette's environment, she can change in ways that suddenly make all the protections you installed inadequate. You've got to keep up with how she's changing so you know what safety features around the house need to be added or adjusted. Like Carter, you've got to be ready to shift the way you think about your baby. You'll get the hang of this, and it will get easier as time passes. The important takeaway from this little lesson is that you shouldn't get too comfortable with the current status quo. Before you change your little dudette's diaper, ask yourself: Is she more prone to rolling away now? Is she able to reach that unlatched drawer? Does your little dude make a beeline for the TV remote whenever you let him go in the living room? Has he started to be attracted to high places?

Your little dude or dudette's safety is in your hands and yours alone. As we've said before and will probably say again, babies don't have brains as we know them. Sure, a zombie will be glad to snack on them, but the babies sure aren't using them for much beyond zombie bait. Yet. Mostly, they're just a bundle of reflexes and urges, wrapped up with a devastatingly cute smile. Which means that you have to do the thinking for them.

Time changes all things, so you have to change with those times. There's only one way to do that:

Be aware. Be alert. Be careful. That way, you won't be sorry.

the dude's guide top 10
your safety checklist at home

You can go onto the Web and find a hundred different places that offer a hundred different lists of things that are essential to making your home safe for your little dude. We like the information that was put out by the U.S. Consumer Product Safety Commission, www.cpsc.gov. They've got a whole section dedicated to simple, easy-to-follow instructions on how you can make anything in your house safer for your little dude. Go there and check out the *Safe Nursery and Childproofing Your Home* publications. They're chock-full of great information.

Or you can simply look at the list we've got below. It's a great starting point for you to begin turning your home from a death trap into a safe space. Make absolutely sure that:

1. the crib is not next to a window, and the mattress is as low as it can go so the little dudette can't easily climb out.

2. any blinds have had their control strings tied up and put out of the way. If you can, change these blinds out for cordless window coverings.

3. everything that can be picked up has been put away.

4. you use safety gates (the kind that have only small openings) to prevent falls down stairs or unwanted entry into unsafe rooms.

5. all corners have been padded and protected.

6. all electrical sockets have been covered over.

7. all doorknobs have been covered, even if that's not necessary. Yet.

8. all cabinet doors are locked shut and cleaning supplies have been moved to a less accessible place.

9. all drawers are locked shut. Unlocked drawers not only allow curious fingers to explore the contents, but they also make for a great stepladder.

10. the refrigerator door and toilet lid are closed and strapped shut. Even the small amount of water in the toilet poses a significant risk of drowning.

the dude's guide top 10
your safety checklist away
from home

You're not always going to be in the safely childproofed nest you call home. There will be times when you have to go outside and bring your little dude with you. Which can make for some disturbing outings, especially if you're going to the home of someone who doesn't have kids. We feel your pain, dudes.

In our opinion, it's best to speak in advance with the friends you'll be visiting and chat them up about what to expect when you bring junior over. Let them know about roving, curious hands and mouths. Then ask if you can lug a few things along to keep your little dude intact — and your friends' furniture, too. In order to make your destination almost as safe as your own home, be sure to take:

1. a pack-and-play crib. It folds up into an easy-to-carry bundle and unfolds into a safe enclosure for your little dude.

2. a few extra electrical-outlet covers.

3. a bouncy chair. You can strap your little dudette into this fabric (nonmotorized) chair, which has bent, elevated supports that allow her to rest or to bounce up and down to her heart's content.

4. a playset and blanket. Set the blanket on the floor, followed by the little dude on his back, followed by the playset. It stands on its own and acts like a mobile, dangling cool, attention-grabbing stuff over his face.

5. eight or 12 corner cushions, just in case that table can't be moved.

6. emergency food and bottles.

7. window guards and doorknob covers.

8. removable cabinet locks and fridge locks.

When you're there:

9. politely ask if you could help them clear away some of the stuff on their lower shelves, stressing that you don't want your child to break anything. Remember to help put things back as well.

10. politely ask if you can move the coffee table out of the room or out of the way.

8

the inside scoop on poop

"oh, my god! what is that?"

Before you even bring your little dude home from the hospital (in fact, within 24 hours after he's born), he's going to have his first poop. It may be just a little different than what you expect. What you're going to find in his diaper is a thick, black or dark-green substance. It's what filled his intestines before he was born, and he's got to pass it out before normal digestion can start up inside there.

A little back story: For the previous 40 (or so) weeks, he's been absorbing all the nutrients and stuff he needs to keep on growing through the umbilical cord, which carries blood and the like in a loop from the mom to the baby and back out again.

He's been swimming in the amniotic fluid all this time. And that's what he swallows when it's time for him to begin practicing swallowing. That stuff will be digested by his tiny, very weak digestive system. However, and this is an important however, if he's healthy, what he won't do is poop any of that stuff out while he's in the womb. For that, he needs to wait until he's out in the big, bright world. That way *you* get to clean it up.

All of which explains something called *meconium*. This is the stuff that's going to try to put you off cleaning poop for the rest of the little dude's life. And it's the very first poop he presents you with. Meconium is the leftovers from digesting nine months' worth of whatever gets swallowed in the womb. It's thick, black, and tarry. It's very sticky and basically looks like every single nightmare vision you've ever had of what poop should *not* look like.

And the worst part is, it's so sticky, it's almost impossible to get off the little dude's butt without you putting in a lot of work. It's like a joke, really. The little dude gives you the worst poop to deal with first, and then eases up on you.

Well, kind of.

After he passes the scary-looking meconium, most times his poop will start to look yellow-green. Sort of. If the little dude is breast-feeding, then his poops should look a little more like light, runny mustard with some tiny seeds in it. Come tell us you still like brown mustard on a hot dog after your little dude has grown out of diapers. We dare you.

The poop will stay runny until he starts to eat solid foods. If your little dude is working off formula, his poops should be more yellow or tan, and they will be a bit more firm than those of a breast-fed kid. However, even if he's bottle-fed, the poops shouldn't be any more firm than, say, creamy peanut butter.

Sorry for ruining peanut butter for you for the next little while. It couldn't be helped.

No matter what your little dude's poop looks like, its color and consistency will change from time to time. It might be because his mom is eating something different and so the breast milk is different, or it might be because he's started on solid foods. Whatever. A little change isn't necessarily a bad thing.

What you need to look out for is the firmness of the poop. If it starts to look hard or dry, it's probably because he's not getting enough liquids. Of course, all that relatively easy stuff goes away once the baby grows older and starts eating real food, but that's for another book.

For now, let's just be thankful that, once the scary-looking meconium goes away, you get to handle some easy poopy diapers. Well, relatively easy, considering you're still wiping poop off a wriggling little butt an astonishingly high number of times every day.

The number of poops your kid has will really be up to him. There's no set number. Some kids have a strong gastrocolic reflex, which means that each time they eat they have to poop and pee. In other kids, not so much. By the time your little dudette is three to six weeks old, if she's breast-fed, she might only have one poop per week, and that's pretty much normal. It's because there's so little waste material in breast milk that the little dudette's digestive system doesn't have much to turn into poop. If your little dudette is taking formula, she ought to be having at least one poop each day. The more the merrier, right?

pop's quiz

the straight poop

1 **Cleanliness is next to . . .**
   A. getting in shape on my list of things that should be done, but we don't have to make a huge deal about it.
   B. perfection, which is over there in the land of make-believe with all the magical unicorns and musical rainbows.
   C. impossible.

2 **You can't hear the game because your little dude is crying so much. He's not hungry. He's not tired, and after you take a quick sniff you rule out that he needs a diaper change. What do you do next?**
   A. Since you always expect a poop, even if the diaper doesn't smell, you lay him down on his back on the changing pad and carefully open the diaper while having a wipe at the ready.
   B. Let him wait a little while longer to make sure he gets good use out of that diaper. They're not cheap, you know?
   C. You set him down on the changing pad on the floor and, keeping your eyes on the TV and the amazing downfield run happening on the screen, you decide to work by feel, right up until the time you wonder what that squishy stuff is.

3 **Changing a little dude is inherently easier, since you're intimately connected with all the equipment down there. How does this affect your prebirth resolution to take your time with every diaper change?**
   A. It doesn't. For one thing, the equipment is upside down and backwards. For another, it's not nearly as under control as the more familiar equipment.
   B. No battle plan survives first contact with the enemy. You know your way around the tackle and don't see the harm in taking a few shortcuts.
   C. What prebirth resolution?

If you answered A for these, you've been paying attention. Good on you! If you answered B, we think you should probably slow down and pay some actual attention, instead of just facing the right direction. If you answered C, you need to reread this chapter — and commit it to memory!

9

turn and
face the
change . . .

diaper training – for you

Once you've brought your little dude home from the hospital, it's more than likely that one of the first things you're going to have to do with him is change his diaper.

Relax. It's going to be easy, provided you're not an idiot.

Richard: *Hi. I'm the idiot mentioned above. When my wife, Alyse, and I brought home our oldest son for the first time, yes, we did have to change him. I volunteered because, well, I needed the brownie points. So, I had Sarcasmo on the changing table, and Alyse stood next to me. I opened the old diaper and, of course, promptly dropped the clean diaper onto the floor. I asked Alyse to hold Sarcasmo still so he didn't fall off the changing table (more on that later), and then I bent down to pick up the diaper. Alyse was feeling the pain of her C-section and not really paying attention beyond making sure the little dude didn't move. While I was down there picking up the clean diaper, I noticed the wall was wet and getting wetter. And I noticed my back was getting wet as well. I was genuinely puzzled about this. It was only when I stood up that I realized that there was a line of pee that went all the way from the opposite wall to Sarcasmo's freshly circumcised penis. So, within five minutes of getting my first son home, I got peed on. Yes, I took that as an omen of things to come.*

Before we go over how to change your little dude, we want to take a moment to remind you that you should have already picked out the main spot where you'll change him, as well as any other decentralized areas you want to set up. Get used to the whole changing process by setting him down and changing him as soon as you can after you get him home.

This next piece of advice is vitally important: When you're changing him anywhere but on the floor, you must *never, ever* take your hand off him. Always keep at least one hand on the little dude's chest, or holding one of his legs. Especially as he gets older, he will be more likely to start juking and jiving and might end up pitching off the table. But if you've got a good grip on him, he's safe as houses.

Still, no matter where you do change him, you'll need to have a changing pad to put him on. You should get one that has not only ridges around the edges so it's harder for him to roll out, but one that also has straps across the middle to hold him in. Make sure these are always fastened to keep your little dude safe. However, you'll find even that is not enough. Despite all these precautions, you still need to make sure you're *always* holding him with one hand.

Okay. So, you've got him home and you've decided to change the little dude first thing. Before you start unlatching and opening the vault, you first need to get ready. Get your wipes and your diapers and an extra set of clothes stacked up nearby, just in case. That way, you won't be searching for anything during the middle of the job.

Mini-Me

Come with us now, into the heart of mystery, into the land of the unfamiliar, as we tell the secrets you're going to wish you'd never even had to consider. Here, then, is how you change a diaper.

What you do is to lift off the sticky tabs on either side of the diaper at the little dude's waist. Most disposable diapers have those. Once you've lifted the tabs, fold them back gently so they're just barely stuck to themselves, and won't reclose. You'll want to make sure they're not sticking tightly because you'll be using them a bit later in the process. Now that the diaper is open, you need to work fast and efficiently. Holding the little dude by the feet and ankles with one hand, lift him up gently, grab the dirty diaper, and set it to the side. Moving even faster, take the clean diaper you've already spread open and put it into place. Remember to not just set it on him. The new diaper also needs to cover his penis. You do not want to get peed on.

Take a wipe and gently clean all around the area where the diaper covered. That means you've got to clean the skin in his groin area, paying special attention to his penis, then wipe his testicles and then around his butt. If it's just a wet diaper, it doesn't really matter in what order you do it. Just remember to cover his penis, with either the diaper or a cloth wipe. Like we said, you do *not* want to get peed on.

Which doesn't mean it's not going to happen to you at some point. As our friend, Carter, can attest.

Carter: *It was terrible.*

I had a handle on changing. After just a few days, I could whip a diaper off, wipe him up, and put a new diaper on him in under 30 seconds consistently. Provided there was no poop. In fact, I was making a bit of a competition out of it.

It was one of those things I would never tell my wife. She wasn't a dude. She wouldn't understand. So I kept the competition to myself and against myself. You know what I'm talking about.

Richard and Barry: *Yes. Yes, we do.*

Barry: *But I know more.*

Richard: *No, I do. I —*

Carter: *So, anyway, there I am whipping through my changing routine with him. The problem was I got so good, I started getting cocky. And when you get cocky, you start cutting corners.*

In this case, I took off the diaper and set it aside. Once I had the diaper out of the way, I wiped him down thoroughly. That's when I really made my mistake.

I know I should have left a wipe over his penis. I should have had a diaper ready to slip over it. I could have done any number of things. But I didn't do any of them.

I just reached for a diaper I had ready. While I was reaching, he started spraying. It was the sound I noticed first since he was . . . pointed . . . away from me. At first, I heard the splashing and I seriously couldn't figure out what it was. I was still puzzled when the first squirt hit me in the face as he was rolling a bit.

My first instinct was to open my mouth in surprise, but I managed to quickly overcome that response, and slammed my mouth closed instead. Then, I reached out and covered him up — with my hands. Now the warm pee was spraying my hands and bouncing back onto him, the changing pad, the carpet, you name it.

How he had that much pee left in him, I'll never know.

I think I taught him a couple of new words that day. When he was done, I figured it was time for a shower for both of us. That was not a fun cleanup, but I have no one to blame but myself.

So when my wife came back from lunch with her friends and asked about a certain odor wafting through the house, I blamed it on the dog.

There's a reason we tell you to do stuff in a certain order, dudes. It's to prevent just this sort of thing from happening to you.

Consider it fair warning.

Another thing to remember is that you're not going to have to deal only with wet diapers. Oh, you'll wish you did, but you won't. (If you're getting a little oogy just reading about the wet diaper, you're going to love Richard's next story.)

If it is a poopy diaper, you need to clean the poop off his butt first, making sure to keep wiping until he's got a spotless behind. Then you get a new wipe and clean the rest of the area. Use as many wipes as you have to. If you use a lot of them at first, don't worry that the cost of wipes is going to wipe you out. You'll get better with practice.

As you're wiping away, be sure to always have something over the little dude's penis when he's not diapered. If that means laying a cloth wipe over it, go ahead. At that age, his penis could be considered a weapon of wet destruction.

Once you've got him cleaned, it's time to seal the diaper. Keeping one hand on his chest or belly, close one side of the diaper at a time. You want to seal the diaper snugly, but not too snugly. If it's too loose, it will come off, and there could be stuff in there you wouldn't want (ahem) leaking out. If it's too tight, not only could stuff squirt out, but, more important, it could cause the little dude some discomfort. Which would make him scream, which would not be fun for either of you.

When you've got the new clean diaper on the little dude and he's taken care of, it's time to dispose of that used diaper. What we're about to tell you is not the only way to take care of it, but it did work for us.

We'd take the used diaper and lay it down on the ground, with the waist section facing away from us. Taking care not to squish anything out, we'd gently roll the diaper up into a cylindrical kind of ball. (You have to take our word, that's what it looks like.) Then we'd unfasten the sticky tabs that we closed gently earlier and stretch them around the rolled-up diaper, making a (somewhat) closed diaper wad.

Now for the fun part: where to put the dirty diaper? You do *not* want to just drop the used diaper into any old trash can in the house. Seriously, dudes. Don't do it. What you need is a plastic-bag-lined trash can that's just for diapers, one that has a top that will close tightly, trapping the odor inside. Once the can is filled, you just take out the full plastic bag and throw it away. Outside. Replace the plastic bag and begin again.

There is also something called a Diaper Genie®, which we hear is a miraculous device for disposing of those pesky dirty diapers.

You Do Not Want a Hat Like This

Richard: *One more little cautionary tale before we move on to discussing the little dudettes. I'd like to introduce you to my friend, whom I'll call, oh, I don't know, Kurt.*

Kurt and his then wife, Peggy, were friends of ours since before college. They were slightly ahead of us in the procreation race in that they actually finished before we even knew there was a race to begin with.

So Kurt and Peggy had their first baby, a lovely little boy born on Halloween. Despite trying his best to give people the impression that he could out-Neanderthal a Neanderthal, Kurt was a progressive little swabbie. Even though he'd never learned how to take care of a baby while on active duty in the Navy, Kurt still thought of himself as a pretty bright guy. After all, the Navy had seen his potential and sent him off to graduate school for some more learning up. How hard could this whole parenting thing be?

One night, Kurt encouraged Peggy to go out with the girls for a little nonbaby fun, confident in the knowledge that he was a smart enough and, gosh darn it, a good enough father that he could take care of his son without having any problems.

He and his son were home alone, and while Kurt was watching some sports program on cable TV, the stench rose up from his young son like a cobra seeking revenge and a particularly plump place to insert its fangs. It wrapped around Kurt's nose and began squeezing.

Kurt decided to change his son's diaper on the carpeted

floor, thinking he was being extra careful. If the little dude fell, there was nowhere he could fall to. Smart move.

What happened next? Not so smart.

Unfortunately for Kurt, it seemed his son was trying for size and volume records. It was a big poop is what I'm saying, and it took a long time and a truly staggering number of baby wipes to get his son clean. About halfway through, Kurt made a rookie mistake. He got distracted.

Kurt dashed off for more wipes, confident that he'd find his young charge still lying on the floor where he'd been left. The problem, you see, is that Kurt had left his son lying next to a huge, poop-filled diaper.

Kurt quickly hustled back to the changing area, but it was too late. His little dude had decided it would be fun to try to wear the used diaper as a hat.

Yep, you read that right.

The little dude had poop running down his head and shoulders and was laughing like it was the funniest thing in the world. Kurt stood still, almost dropping the wipes from his numb fingers. A wave of horror washed over him, draining all the blood from his face. And the little dude kept laughing, having more fun than he'd ever thought possible.

Eventually, Kurt snapped out of it and grimly walked over to his son, picked him up, and walked him to the bathroom, where the bathtub waited. Kurt figured it would be easier to hose off his son and then set about cleaning up the carpet. Kurt can laugh about it now, but back then, he would shudder whenever anyone brought it up. So, take a lesson from our friend, Kurt, and don't leave dirty diapers in easy reach of your little dude.

Nooks and Crannies

For most dudes, getting to see a vagina has been something of a holy quest since they hit puberty. Well, if you've got a little dudette, you're going to be seeing a lot of that in the years to come, but it's going to be a totally different experience. And, boy, is it going to feel strange. No question about that.

You're going to have to become totally familiar with your daughter's vagina, labia, and butt. Just because she's a girl doesn't mean you won't have to change her. And when you change her, you're going to have to look closely and make sure she is really, *really* clean.

Because pee comes out a lot closer to everything else on girls, they're more likely to get urinary tract infections if they don't stay clean, and, dude, that's *your* job.

For starters, no matter if it's a poopy diaper or just a wet diaper, you always have to wipe from the front to the back. That is, you need to start at the top of her labia and wipe down past her anus. This is because you don't want any particles of poop to get into her vagina, where it can more easily cause an infection and diaper rash.

You've also got to make sure you really clean all the nooks and crannies down there. Most babies are pretty roly-poly and have rolls of fat along their legs and butts. When you hold up their legs, that fat will bunch up. On girls, who already have more canyons than peaks, it's especially important that you spread apart all the little fat rolls and wipe them down (going front to back, remember?) thoroughly.

Acting Rashly

Let's talk about diaper rash. That's the irritation that happens to the skin mostly covered by a diaper. The most common signs of diaper rash are redness or little red bumps on the abdomen, genitals, butt, and thighs in areas that have been in contact with a wet or poopy diaper.

The most common cause of diaper rash is leaving a wet or pooped-out diaper on your baby for too long. Moisture from a wet diaper causes the skin to be too easily chafed. Digestive agents in the poop can start to attack your kid's skin if the poopy diaper isn't changed promptly. Either way, the baby's not happy. And if the baby's not happy, you're not happy.

No matter how the rash starts, once the skin is irritated, it gets easier and easier to irritate it some more by further contact with pee or poop. We've found that the best way to deal with it is to thoroughly clean the area and then cover it with a diaper-rash cream that contains zinc oxide. This will keep liquids away from the irritated skin, while giving it a chance to heal.

If your kid has diaper rash, try to change her diaper more frequently so you can reduce her exposure to pee and poop. Also, try to expose her bottom to the air as much as possible, which means putting her diapers on a little more loosely than normal so the air can circulate around in there. You should also change the diaper as soon as possible when she poops.

pop's quiz

home alone

1. **No matter how much you try to avoid it, there will come a day, a day like no other, when you will be left alone with your little dudette. It will be just you and her, with no other adult around to supervise. Don't panic. We're certain you're ready for this moment. But, just to make sure, let's go over a few scenarios.**

    A. Since you know your little dudette habitually wakes up around 6 a.m., you set your alarm for 5:30 a.m., so you can be wide awake and ready to go when she is.

    B. You set it for 9:30 a.m., because it's the weekend and you deserve to sleep in a little for once.

    C. Alarm? Alarms are for wimps. Besides, you're too nervous about the coming day to even think about getting sleep.

2. **Your little dudette is still eating only breast milk, but has shown she will take either the bottle or the breast; as long as it's her mother's milk, she's fine. What do you do about feeding her on your big day alone with her?**

    A. Ask your wife to try to set aside enough milk to get your daughter through the day, and remind her that it's a small price to pay for getting a day off.

    B. Breast milk? Feh. You've got the same delivery system. All you need is some hormones and you're good to go. You think you saw some kind of hormone pills in your wife's medicine cabinet.

    C. Breast milk? Does it have to be *human* breast milk? Because you know where there's a cow or two who are willing to look the other way for a discreet tug and a couple of bucks.

3 You're not going to waste any time when you've got your day with the little dudette. You want to get out and do stuff with her. Plus, you've heard that nothing attracts the women like carrying around a cute baby. How do you get ready to take her out for the day?

A. You go through your checklist, making sure to have ample food, a full diaper bag, a comprehensively researched itinerary with times and directions, and enough money to get you through the day.

B. You think you read somewhere in the paper about a baby event somewhere uptown. It shouldn't be too hard to find.

C. You carefully store the inch-thick sheaf of printouts you've compiled for the stated objective of the day, followed by three fallback positions, a wild card, and a potluck objective. There's just enough room for the printouts next to the minifridge holding her three gallons of breast milk in refrigerated comfort. You're sure you'll be able to squeeze the car seat in there somewhere.

If you picked A as your response to these questions, you get to go to the head of the class. If B was your answer of choice, then you should probably answer the imaginary phone ringing in your head, because the residents of CrazyLand want their king back on the throne. If you stuck to C for your answers, we're pretty sure your brain is stuck somewhere, too. Ground control to Major Dad, can you hear us??

10

's not a
pretty sight

being nosy

Raising little dudes and dudettes is a dirty business, but somebody's got to do it.

Let's not even mention the poop and the pee and the spit-up. Well, technically, we suppose it's a bit late for that, considering we've devoted entire chapters to some of that stuff already, but work with us here. It's hard writing a book.

In this chapter, we're going to take a shot at writing about snot. Get used to it.

Healthy mucus is clear and functions as a dirt trap in your nose, filtering out the dust and junk in the air. Which, by the way, is where boogers come from. Boogers are just mucus mixed with dirt and other airborne stuff. (Ah, the little nuggets you learn when you're not even expecting it.)

Anyway, here's the thing about snot. We adults take care of snot a couple of ways. Either we blow it out using a tissue, or we pick it out using a finger. (It's okay. We've all done it.)

Little dudes, however, can't do either. When they get a nose full of snot, all they can do is scream and cry about it. Which, of course, just makes it worse. When the little dude is so young, you can't get him to blow the snot out into a tissue. And we're reasonably sure *you* don't want to pick his nose clean either.

What we recommend using is a suction bulb (called by some a "snot sucker") that's filled with a little saline water. Picture a turkey baster. A suction bulb is basically the soft, squeezy rubber part of the turkey baster, only it comes to a relatively short, narrow point. When your little dude has a stuffed nose, use a suction bulb to gently squirt some warm saline water into his nose, while making sure his head is upright.

The saline water will loosen and dry the blocked snot. (It's the salt in the saline water that will dry up the mucus membranes.) Then, you use another suction bulb to, well, suck all the goop out of his nose. After that, repeat as necessary. Make sure you label each bulb, not only with the little dude's name (especially if you've got more than one), but also with "saline" and "snot" on each. That way you won't get mixed up and accidentally shoot snot into your little dude's nose.

It won't be a pleasant experience for either you or your little dude, but it's definitely better than him trying to breathe through a completely stuffed-up nose.

You can clean out the snotsucker by filling the sink with warm, soapy water. Squeeze the bulb, insert the open end into the water, and release the bulb. That will suck up the soapy water into the bulb. Cover the opening and swish around. Squirt until it's empty and repeat.

Crusty Eyes

Of course, eyes get boogers as well. We're sure you've experienced the crusty, hard mucus that forms in the corners of your eyes. Little dudes and dudettes get that stuff as well.

And, as always, you're the one who gets to clean it up.

Make sure you clean gently around the little dude's eyes with a warm washcloth and some water. That should just about do it.

However, there is another reason to keep an eye (no pun intended) on the little dude's eyelids. It's something called conjunctivitis, which is also known as pinkeye and is extremely contagious.

> **Barry:** *I once got pinkeye as an adult for no apparent reason. None of my little dudes had it. No one in their preschool classes had it. No one we knew had it. But I still somehow managed to get it. Which just proves that it's hard to be on your guard with something that's so contagious.*

The most visible symptoms of pinkeye are, of course, a bloodshot eyeball and an extremely crusty eyelid, almost completely covered in eye boogers. If your little dude has these symptoms, again, use the warm, wet washcloth to clear away his eyelids so he can at least see. Once you've done that, make sure to thoroughly wash your own hands and then throw the washcloth into the washing machine. Contagious, remember?

After cleaning the little dude off, the very next thing you need to do is to call your pediatrician. Make an appointment to get the little dude in as soon as possible. Pinkeye, though a pain in the butt, is also completely treatable with medication.

11

let sleeping babies lie

welcome to zombieville . . .

Imagine that for nine months, you never see the sun and you never see light. Imagine that unending darkness is all that you know. Pretty depressing, huh? Well, you don't have to imagine it. You did experience it. You and every baby everywhere.

When a baby is in her mother's womb, she doesn't see any light until she's born. Because of that, she doesn't have any idea what day or night are. She doesn't know that when that big, bright ball in the sky is up there, people are supposed to be up and walking around and doing all the interesting stuff that people do. She doesn't know that when there isn't any big, round ball brightly shining up there, it's called night, and that's the time when people are quiet and sleeping and far less interesting.

To her, it's all the same, no matter what time it is. And lucky you — you get to teach her the difference between day and night, and when it's the right time to sleep and the right time to be awake. Fortunately, your little dudette will be right there with you, making sure you do a good job teaching.

When she first gets home, your little dudette will have a stomach capable of only holding about two to three hours' worth of food at a time. So, really, there's no escaping the fact that she will be waking you up like clockwork all through the night. But you can start to teach her that nighttime is for sleeping, even when you have to feed her.

When she wakes up at night, try to keep the feeding as quiet and as soothing as possible. If you can, don't turn on any lights and don't play with her during the feeding. And, if you're feeding her, you'll have to change her. Be as speedy and gentle as possible when you're doing a nighttime changing. Then, when you're done feeding, changing, and burping her, put her back down in her crib as quickly as possible and leave the room.

She might cry a little and, depending on your parenting style, you can either try to go in and do a little comforting, or you can let her soothe herself and eventually go back to sleep.

> **Richard:** *Our first son, Sarcasmo, slept in the same room as my wife and I did. We had borrowed a bassinet from a friend, thinking that it would be nice to have him in the same room. We assumed it would be easier since I wouldn't have to get up and go get the little dude for my wife to feed him. Or my wife wouldn't have to get up and stumble into the little dude's room to feed him.*
>
> *What we didn't realize is that we would have him in the same room as us.*
>
> *I know that seems a bit odd, but it's the truth. We were concentrating only on convenience. That it would be easier for me to walk around the bed than to bounce off hallway walls toward the little dude's room and hope I managed a straight line on the way back.*

We were of the firm belief that we shouldn't run to the little dude every time he made a noise, because we wanted him to be able to comfort himself back to sleep at some point in his life. We could just see a teenager wandering into our room demanding a story or a glass of water before he went back to bed. So, our plan was, unless he was in full-throated crying mode, demanding a change or more fuel, we would let him go. We had a plan.

However, what we didn't count on was that Sarcasmo wasn't a completely silent baby. Like all tots, he made little sighs, small peeps, sheet-rustling noises, and other bits of parent-waking sounds. The low-level sonic assault continued at all hours, for every second he wasn't up and screaming for more food or to be changed.

Since we were literally only inches away from him, we got to hear everything. And, being paranoid new parents, it seemed like every single time Sarcasmo moved, it would wake us up. I'd jolt awake, sure that something horrible had happened. I'd listen for anything over the sound of my hammering heart, and then finally convince myself it was nothing, and go back to sleep. Only to be jolted awake again by another little peep.

It was an ugly situation. And that's not even talking about what I saw every morning when I looked in the mirror. Yikes!

Of course, as time went on, we did get better at it. That is to say, we got better at not sweating the small stuff.

Our second son didn't get the bassinet. Our friend needed it back, so we brainstormed and came up with the idea of putting some sheets tightly over some egg-crate padding, and then laying Zippy the Monkey Boy on top of the padding in a laundry basket. Which worked awesomely well. That was one fantastic laundry basket. Almost two decades later, we still have it and use it.

By the time our third son arrived, we'd moved into a new house and had room to spread out. Hyper Lad, already living up to his nickname, was a restless little dude. When he was one month old, we put him in his own room and set up a baby monitor.

And then we promptly slept through the entire night, completely ignoring all his yelling and screaming. Bad parents, indeed. We managed to refocus enough to get back on track, making sure we did actually wake up for the big things. For the little things, though, we just let it slide.

Remember, it was a plan. It wasn't something we did just because we were tired. That, at least, is our story and we're sticking with it.

You can also do a little sleep training by not letting her nap too much during the late afternoon. If she's not tired at night, she won't sleep. It's as simple as that. We're not saying you should keep her up all the time, but playing with her during the late afternoon instead of letting her get a four-hour snooze would probably be a good thing.

If you and your partner decide the little dudette is going to be breast-fed, you're still not off the hook. Sure, your partner is going to be doing most of the work, but you'll be needed for support stuff. If that means helping to change the baby after feeding or doing anything your partner demands so she can get back to sleep more easily, well, that's your job.

Which means you're going to have to be at least semi-awake whenever feeding time rolls around. We're sure that you and your wife will work out what each of you needs to be doing when the little dude wakes up each night, but that's negotiable. The one thing you have to remember is to do everything as quietly as possible. To your little dude, noise means happy, happy fun time, which means he should be awake and laughing and not missing out on all the good stuff by sleeping.

During your little dude's early days at home, you'll be devoting a large amount of time to teaching his infant body what it should be doing, which includes sleep. You can help with that learning process by making sure you curse silently when you stub your toe in the darkness, or walk nose-first into a wall.

pop's quiz

the sleep of the just (or just go to %$!ç†© sleep)

1. **You're tired and find yourself nodding off with your sleeping little dude in your arms. What do you do?**
   - A. Put him in his crib, and then find a nearby place for you to sleep.
   - B. Duct tape your arms around your little dude so you can't drop him, and then fall asleep in your chair.
   - C. Ask the bartender for the check, and then apologize for all the drool on the bar.

2. **It's one of your favorite times of the day: naptime. To help prepare your little dudette for her sleep, do you . . .**
   - A. turn down lights and put on some soft music by Al Green, followed by her afternoon bottle and an uncluttered space in her rocking crib?
   - B. turn down the volume on the television . . . slightly?
   - C. light some scented candles and ply her with a tall, cold glass of chocolate milk?

3. **You still have vague memories of when you used to be able to sleep through the night. These memories keep taunting you, and you're determined to get another good night's sleep, and soon. What do you do?**
   - A. Man up and tough it out. You've got a schedule and a plan you should stick to, so you can help your little dudette start sleeping through the night on her own.
   - B. Tell your wife about this really important convention you've got to go to in, um, Weehawken.
   - C. Baby monitor? What baby monitor? And no, I don't know why the door to our bedroom is locked and bolted and the space between the door and the floor is lined with cushions and blankets. Still, it looks like a lot of work to change it, so why not get it in the morning?

If you answered A to these questions, then you've got a good handle on how to get through the night. If you answered B, that makes us wonder if you actually read the questions and answers. If you answered C, we're guessing it was because that was the one you always picked in college when you didn't know the answer. Come on, you seriously picked C?

The Right Position

No matter what you might have heard, you should not put your little dude on his stomach when it's time to sleep. For years, people thought that letting babies sleep on their stomachs was the safest way to go. However, recent research shows that it's much safer, particularly as a means of preventing Sudden Infant Death Syndrome (SIDS), for babies to sleep on either their sides or their backs.

According to a recent publication by the American Academy of Pediatrics, SIDS is the leading cause of death for babies between one month and 12 months old, with the greatest frequency in the first four months. While no one is sure what causes babies to die of SIDS, there are a few simple steps you can take that will drastically reduce your little dude's chances of dying from it. The most obvious step is to have your little dude sleep in a crib on his back.

One recent study that we read (so you wouldn't have to) suggests that this might be a safer position because of something to do with the gasp reflex. We all stop breathing occasionally — it's scary, but true. Still, our brains know what to do. They trigger this little reflex and we gasp back to breathing. SIDS could possibly be a failure of that reflex. No one really knows. It's a bit frightening, but that should help you remember to get your little dude in the habit of sleeping on his back.

The best place for your baby to sleep, according to the AAP, is in your room, but not in your bed. We're not passing judgment on co-sleeping (the practice of your baby sleeping in the bed with you), but only passing along what the AAP says.

The joint recommendation of the AAP is that you put

your little dudette in a crib or bassinet in your room. Make sure there are no toys, soft coverings, blankets, pillows, or anything in the crib with her. Kind of a shocker, we know. The AAP wants you to put your darling little girl to bed with no blanket to tuck her in? Yep, it really does. We also want to mention that the crib should not have bumper pads as they would pose a suffocation danger. And we want to remind you to make sure that the sheet covering the mattress is *tightly* secured.

However, there are pretty good alternatives to loose blankets. For instance, you could put her in sleep sacks (wearable blankets or sleepers), which are baby clothes specially designed for nighttime. We think it's worth giving up a few expectations of what you thought bedtime would look like to keep your baby safe.

We realize that you couldn't get through a night without your pillows propping up your head, that pillow under your arm, maybe another between your knees. . . . But that's you. You're an adult. Your little dudette is a baby, and she should not be around pillows when she's sleeping. She could toss and turn and end up wedged under a pillow, and that would be very bad. She's perfectly comfortable sleeping on her back on a firm mattress. She likes it, so don't worry.

These recommendations are for babies up to one year. The period of maximum danger from dying of SIDS should be over by the time they turn six months, which, coincidentally, is about when they start learning to turn over on their own, but it's always a good idea to have her start out sleeping on her back. So, initially, for naptime and nighttime your little dudette should always sleep on her back, in her crib or bassinet, in your room.

The Cover-Up

Since we're not going to be using blankets or other cover-ups, you might want to make sure to purchase your little dude something warm to sleep in. Preferably something with feet on the end of the legs. Or sleep sacks, which we mentioned in the preceding section.

Footie pajamas are more than just a really cool-looking thing to wear (although, possibly, not for adults, so move on there, dude), they're also extremely practical. Even when it's okay to have blankets in the crib (after one year, remember?), it's still a good idea to dress your little dude in footie pajamas. He's going to be squirming around like a hyperactive snake on hot sand. No matter how nice the blanket, he won't stay snuggled under it.

Since you're not going to be giving him blankets anyway, get him started wearing footie pajamas right from the beginning. He stays warm. He looks good. And you don't have to worry. As much.

The Good News

Most babies (the most reliable figure is 90 percent) will be sleeping six to eight hours without waking up by the time they are three months old. (Of course, you being the conscientious parents you are and having woken up with him every single night for those at-least three months, it's probably going to feel like it's been three years since the little dude arrived. Relative time is nothing like real time. Sorry.) Mostly, this depends on the size of the little dude. Once he hits 12 to 13 pounds, his stomach will be able to hold enough food so that he can sleep longer without waking up hungry.

So if your little dude is a big little dude, he might be sleeping through the night a little earlier than three months.

Here's the thing — *the* thing — that really gets to us about sleeping and babies and parents and all of that: No matter how little sleep the little dude gets during the night, he's *always* chipper and ready to go in the morning. *Plus* he gets to take naps during the day.

Whereas we dads (and, we guess, some moms as well, though definitely not *our* kids' moms) fall out of bed in the morning looking like someone spent the intervening evening smacking the tar out of them with the ugly stick that got its start making warthogs look presentable. Hair, if there's any left, is shooting off in a thousand different directions. The bags under each eye are big enough that we'd get charged twice if we tried to check them in at an airline counter. And, until that coffee or Coke hits the bloodstream and begins battering away at the doors of the brain, our cognitive skills are still somewhere on the stupid side of a sack of hammers.

And then we have to go to work all day — except for those short micronaps that always culminate in us jerking awake like someone hit us with a cattle prod when we start falling off the chair.

We think you get the picture. It's not fun.

And here's the other thing. It's not going to get much better for a while. You might as well resign yourself to the fact that you're pretty much going to be tired most days. Or, as was the case for our friend Jude, about five years.

Jude: *Looking back, I really don't remember all that much of the first five years raising our three boys.*

Mostly what I remember is being so tired. All the time. It's all a big blur of diapers and wipes and burp rags and warm bottles and baby food and spilled Cheerios.

I think we might have brought home a dog somewhere in there, because we have one now and I'm pretty sure I remember yelling at someone while pointing at a puddle of pee.

Being tired is tough, especially when you're trying to think things through, but it can be done. I remember when my sons got old enough that they were sleeping through the night and I didn't have to do a diaper change every seven minutes or so. . . . It was so strange. I felt weirdly energetic: I wasn't always dropping or losing my car keys. I knew where stuff was. And the carpet stopped trying to trip me whenever I walked over it. It took me a while, but I finally realized I wasn't tired. And it was a revelation.

Which was just about the time my wife started talking about how she wished she had a daughter.

So, yeah. It's something you're going to have to get used to feeling.

Still, that feeling when you first get to sleep through the night again . . . It's so very wonderful. Even if you used to need nine hours of sleep to feel like you were approaching the idea of being human, you'll find that the first six-hours-in-a-row night of uninterrupted sleep is amazing.

When that happened to Richard, the first thing he did was to jump up out of bed and race to his little dude's room, convinced that something horrible had happened to him during the night. Nope, the kid just decided to get a good night's sleep.

12

you-haul . . .
a lot

road trip! bag the beer, but bring the bottles

Remember those days, long ago, when you could pop out to the grocery store to get a couple of things and be back in 20 minutes? You do? Well, forget it. Those days are long gone, dude.

Now that the little dudette has arrived, she's going to introduce you to an Einsteinian time-suck that obliterates black holes. That is, you'll find that all time is relative. Your little dudette will make sure that every 20-minute errand takes one hour. Every ten-minute pit stop will take one hour. Every time you get into the car with her, it will take at least one hour.

In fact, having her will make every errand you run take about two to three times longer than it used to. But, that's okay. You need to resign yourself to the fact that it's going to take a lot of time and that you're not going to rush. If you rush, you can do stupid things like leave her in the car or get into an accident or even forget why you went out in the first place. Instead, just enjoy your time with her. It's a cliché, but it's a cliché because it's true: they do grow up very, very fast. She will never be one month old again.

Instead of worrying that the errand is taking too long, when you stop to park, turn around and play footsie with her. Sure, that will take up a bit more time, but she will laugh and smile and, dude, that's cool.

Hauling Ass Takes Two Loads
or
Hurry Up and Finish Packing, We Leave in Three Days

Being in a relationship, you know that women can pack a whole lot of stuff when they go on long trips. Well, having a baby means that what women pack is really nothing compared to what you're going to have to bring along for the little dude.

To start with, you'll have to pack at least three different outfits for him for each day. You might not use them all, but if you don't bring the extra clothes, the gods of karma will make sure that he not only wets through his outfit, but has a blowout poop as well.

In addition to clothes, you'll have to re-create his room in its entirety. That is, you'll have to bring another set of just about everything you use at home. There are baby wipes, spare diapers, more spare diapers, a crib for him to sleep in, more baby wipes, bottles (if you use them), even more spare diapers, toys (not so much to amuse him on the ride, since that'll be your job, but to make that job of yours a little easier), any type of medicine he might conceivably need for any situation short of an emergency-room visit, a cooler to store breast milk for bottles, something in which to heat the breast milk when he's hungry, even more baby wipes, burp rags, a changing pad, and about 15 other things that we've probably forgotten. (For all those things, see "The Dude's Guide Top 10 Safety Checklist Away from Home" on page 89).

That's okay. The first couple of times you go on a trip with him, you will forget something. The next trip, you'll remember the first thing you forgot, but will forget the first thing you remembered last time. Don't let it discourage you. Just keep trying. Eventually you'll get it right.

"Minivans Are Cool"

If we keep saying that enough times, maybe people will start believing it's true.

> **Richard:** *What? Of course they are. Of course they are. Of course they are.*

It's not like we're telling you to ask directions, or anything horrible like that.

We kid you not — even walking to the curb to check the mailbox can turn into an adventure if your little dude suddenly needs to get changed. So going somewhere that's not within sprinting distance from your home? That requires some forethought and some packing. And the self-confidence to pull off something truly different.

You're going to have to have a diaper bag.

The first thing we're suggesting is that your family has at least two diaper bags. One can be for your wife, and that can be as cute (or not) as she wants to make it. It will have all the pouches and spaces and detachable changing pads and temperature-resistant pockets to keep the cold side cold and the hot side hot. We wouldn't be surprised if it even has Wi-Fi and Bluetooth.

The thing of it is, no matter how tricked out it is with all the latest gadgets, there's almost no chance you're going to be able to go outside with that thing over your shoulder and still call yourself any kind of a dude. Sorry, but it's true. And that's coming from a couple of dudes who think they look good in pink.

Unfortunately, most makers of diaper bags that are designed to carry stuff like spare diapers, baby wipes, extra clothes, bottles, etc., think in terms of frilly flowers and pretty pinks and rainbows and stars. They don't think about footballs or baseballs, or balls period. They also don't think about the different sizes between men and women. Women, generally, are smaller. Men, generally, are larger. For example, we need longer straps to carry all this stuff comfortably.

Of course, can we really be comfortable while we're carrying something more suited to a 12-year-old girl? Probably not. That's why we suggest you come up with your own solution to carrying all the baby stuff.

The first thing you'll need to do is to go out to some place that sells cheap men's clothing and buy as many pairs of cargo- pocket shorts and cargo-pocket pants as you can afford. Make sure they're cheap, because they will get stuff on them that you won't believe.

Richard: *This is so very true. Once I had kids, I started living in cargos. In fact, that's still a major source of tension between me and She Who Has Her Own Fashion Opinions. She wants me to wear something other than cargos, but I don't have them. Cargo pockets are just too darn useful. Especially when you carry around a five-pound wallet. Mine started to weigh that much* *when I replaced the condoms with all the pictures I need to be a properly equipped dad.*

Barry: *Personally, I like clothes that are less absorbent. That way, the spills that happen, and oh they will happen, won't leave too many stains. I like stuff like sweatsuits made from microfiber materials and even those new pants that are stain resistant.*

Depending on your little dudette's age, you can almost get by with only cargo pockets to carry your stuff. Use the normal pockets for your wallet and keys and such. Use the cargos for baby stuff.

Richard: *What I did was to use one cargo pocket for diapers, wipes, and ziplock bags. I used the other cargo pocket for a change of clothes and the bottle. That way, I could warm the bottle before we left, then wrap it in the clothes for insulation, and it would keep warm.*

If your little dudette needs a bit more stuff than that, we suggest you go out and get yourself a sturdy backpack. Not the we're-going-on-a-three-week-European-trip-size backpack, but a good-sized one. It's got to have a variety of different pockets, or compartments from large to small. Because you will be stuffing them to the gills. Once you've got that packed, keep it next to the door so you'll have it ready whenever you need it. Lately, we've also been hearing that some dudes like using messenger bags to schelp around diaper-changing materials. So, you have a couple of options. If you do break down and decide to get a diaper bag (or if one of your friends gives you one as a present), turn the page for our suggestions about what to put in it.

our top 13 list of what every dude should have in the diaper bag
or
"they're very big in europe"

1. Plenty of correctly sized diapers. You'd be surprised how often we forgot that our little dudette was growing, and when it came time to change her we'd have diapers that were too small. A diaper meant for a 20-pound baby doesn't exactly fit one who weighs 35 pounds. Take our word for it.

1a. a gallon-sized re-sealable plastic bag to dispose of dirty diapers (for a very short time) or for putting smelly clothes aside until you can wash them

2. More wipes than you think you could possibly need. The good news is that wipes come in travel packs that keep them moist. But they're not perfect. Make sure you check the moisture level of the wipes before you head out. Replace if dry.

3. a replacement binky or two

4. A changing pad big enough for the little dude. You don't want to change him on the ground or on the carpet in the back of your minivan. One will get him dirty, and one will get your stuff dirty. Either way, bad idea.

5. A change of clothing that fits the little dudette. It's not a deal breaker, but you probably don't want to cart her around in just her diaper.

6. Several ziplock plastic bags for storage of, shall we say, dirty clothing. You don't want that stuff inside the minivan with you.

7. Sunscreen. Babies have delicate skin, and you need to protect them, so buy sunscreen made for them, not for adults.

8. Diaper-rash cream. Babies have delicate skin, and you . . . oh, you know.

9. Burp cloths. Check out the range of cloths available — from terry to hemp to organic cotton.

10. Food and plenty of it. Make sure you have prewarmed formula in bottles, if that's the little dude's gig, or breast milk. Food is *essential*.

11. toys or something shiny to hold her attention for a little bit

12. Meds. If your little dude's sick, make sure you have his medication. If he's well, make sure to have some pain reliever on hand anyway. Just in case.

13. Cash. Just enough to cover emergencies in case you lose your wallet, or forget to bring it, or leave it in the car. Trust us, babies take up a lot of your brain, so there's not as many gray cells left to focus on frivolous stuff like wallets. And remember to put your name, address, and phone number on the diaper bag, because we guarantee you it will get lost at least once.

As your baby gets older, the list of essentials will begin to drop. Of course, you'll have to start packing different things as well, such as goldfish crackers and bright, shiny items your child will find entertaining.

The big takeaway here is to remember to check the contents of your diaper bag on a regular basis. Diapers and wipes need to be replenished, and other items should be restocked to keep up with usage and with the little dudette's growth. You want to make sure that the wipes are still wet and the diapers are still the right size. Restock right after you come back from a trip. That way, you won't forget any essentials for your next trip out.

the naked truth about baby skin

a few tips on keeping him soft

There's an old expression about how something is as soft and smooth as a baby's butt. Well, there's a reason for that saying, and the reason is that a baby's skin is just about the softest thing you'll ever feel. Just because it's soft, though, doesn't mean there can't be some things that go wrong with it.

For starters, your little dude's skin might get dry. The most common cause for a little dude to have dry skin is that he's being bathed too much. We know that sounds strange, but it's true. When you wash a baby, not only do you wash away dirt, you also wash away essential oils that keep his skin soft.

During the first year or so, as long as you wash the little dude's genital area thoroughly each time you change his diaper, there's really no need for you to give him a bath more than about once or twice a week. That's assuming the little dude doesn't get himself covered in poop or pee. If that happens, it's straight to the bathtub.

If your little dude starts getting dry skin, there are a few other things you can do to help. For one, put a humidifier in his room. This will pump more moisture into the air, which will be good for his skin. You can also use a baby lotion on the dry areas. The best way to do this is to use a small amount of good-quality lotion right after giving him a bath. Finally, try using *less* soap during baths. Most soaps have drying agents and only rarely need to be used on small babies, except around the genitals.

She Can't Be a Teenager Yet

Even though your little dudette is only a couple of months old, she can still get acne. Yep, you read that right. Babies are not immune to getting zits.

Sometimes, some little dudettes will get whiteheads on their faces and occasional whiteheads on their abdomens or arms and legs. These form because the little oil glands in the skin get clogged. The best way to treat them is to ignore them. They will go away on their own. Just keep those areas clean.

Whiteheads aren't the only skin problems your little dudette might face. No pun intended. She might get what is called infant acne. As in the case of regular teenage acne, the cause is hormones. Unlike with teenagers, though, the hormones causing acne in your little dudette don't belong to her. These hormones belong to her mom. They are still washing around in the little dudette's system, wreaking havoc on her skin.

Again, don't worry about it all that much. Just wash the acne area with water a couple of times a day and pat it dry, and the acne will go away on its own after a few months. Even better, there should be no lasting scars.

No Waitin' on a Sunny Day . . .

It's tons of fun to take your little dude out into the park on a sunny day, walk out in the fresh air, and introduce him to the great outdoors. But there's something you need to do every time you get ready to take him outside. You need to cover him in sunscreen — even if it's a cloudy day, because the sun's rays are dangerous even when it's overcast. The invisible ultraviolet rays are still churning and hitting everyone who ventures out.

This is not something to take lightly. Studies have shown that getting a sunburn early in life can drastically increase your chances of getting skin cancer later on. The best thing to do is to try to keep him out of the sun between 10 a.m. and 2 to 3 p.m., which is when there are the most ultraviolet rays about.

If you can't keep him out of the sun, you need to make sure you always cover him in sunscreen with at least a 15 SPF (sun protection factor). If the little dude has fair skin, he should get a sunscreen with at least a 30 SPF. And remember that even water-resistant sunscreens will wash off. If you and the little dude are out in the sun for a long time, remember to reapply the sunscreen every two hours or so.

You should also make sure the little dude is wearing lightweight clothes with long sleeves and long pants. If it's too hot for that, make sure to reapply sunscreen on exposed limbs fairly often.

If you don't think you'll find a shady spot, bring a beach umbrella or something similar to make your own shade. And, to complete the ensemble, have the little dude wear a hat with a brim wide enough to shade his face and ears.

mommy magnet

how to survive carrying the center of attention in your arms

If we didn't know any better, we'd think little dudes were much smarter than we give them credit for. They'd have to be, even if all they wanted to do was survive.

Let's face it, there are times your baby will drive you crazy, exasperate you, and cause you endless nights of worry, but one of the things that makes it all worth it is, you guessed it . . .

They're sooooo cuuuuuute!

We think they do it on purpose. We can't tell you how many times we've been jolted awake by the cries of a little dude we were sure was going to sleep through the night, or at least the next three hours. We were about to do our best impression of the Grinch, only to get gobsmacked by the charisma radiating from the crib. That cute smile, evident even when he's screaming.

The way his forehead squinches up just so.

The beautiful, almost angelic look of peace and contentment as he burbles back to sleep. It doesn't matter how annoyed we are, because as soon as we see even a smidgen of that cuteness, all that is forgotten and we're under his spell. Again.

We're both fairly certain that this X Factor in babies is pretty much why we continue making more babies — they're the true dominant species on the planet. We exist to care for them, and we don't mind it. Sometimes, though, there can be benefits to having that kind of magnetism on your side.

When you go out with the little dude, you are going to be a bit of a health hazard. We all know that zombies can sometimes walk the Earth. We mean, what dude hasn't seen and loved *Dawn of the Dead*? Right? Of course you have.

Well, you and the little dude are about to start creating your own zombies, and they're all going to be women. There's something about little dudes and dudettes that tends to turn off the brains of most women and make them crave the cuteness that is baby.

Get ready to be surrounded by women wearing slack-jawed looks of incomprehension as they notice the little bundle in your arms, but instead of mumbling for "Braaaaaiiiiiiiiins," they'll be cooing, "Baaaaaabbbbbby."

We know you thought you were handsome before, but with the addition of the little dude, you'll be irresistible. Of course, you're also probably in a committed relationship, if not married, so it won't do you much good. But, hey, this newfound attention is still not a bad thing.

> **Barry:** *If I'd have known kids would attract as many women as they have, I would have had kids a long time ago. Or at least borrowed a few.*

Barry's just kidding. The fact is, for all the women who started coming up to us because of the gurgling, sweet baby in our arms, none of them could hold a candle — in terms of charisma, charm, beauty, and brains — to the women we had already found and made part of our lives.

Richard: *The thing is, this sort of magnetism doesn't work only on relative strangers in the park. It also works on relatives, but in a different way. Carrying a cute little grandkid can render you temporarily invisible. I was the oldest grandson on my side of the family, so I was always the center of attention. Of course. Then I became a dad. As soon as that happened, I went from being the apple of my grandparents' eyes to a transport system for their adorable center of the universe.*

clothes make the baby

"who put her in that?"

We're not here to tell you what styles of clothing to choose for your little dude or dudette. Come on, we're dudes. That choice, friends, is really up to you.

> **Richard:** *However, let me just say that I think all sailor suits should be banned permanently and purged from our global memory and retail inventory. But that's just a personal thing.*

What we do want to discuss is not how clothes look, but how they function.

> **Barry:** *Looks have nothing to do with it. I need clothing that works on my daughter. Looks are something her mother worries about, not me.*

There are some baby shorts, pants, or pajama bottoms that are one continuous piece. That is, they're just like adult bottoms. If you want to take them off your little dude or dudette, you have to slip them down over wriggling legs. When you're in a hurry because there's some sort of gas attack coming from the diaper and it looks like something's about to explode, it's not that easy to whip those kinds of bottoms off.

We recommend pants, shorts, and pajamas that have snaps running all the way up both inseams. These snaps can be quickly undone, and the pants whipped up over the waist so you've got quick access to the diaper. Then, when you're done, you just pull down the pants and snap them up again. It's quick and relatively painless.

Some clothes you'll dress your kid in are actually a bit difficult to figure out.

> **Barry:** *One time, I put my youngest daughter in this nice dress that had a cute collar and some buttons running down the back. As soon as my wife walked in, she started laughing, because, she said, "You put that dress on backwards."*

Which, we think, is acceptable. Women, you see, have an innate sense for clothing. It's a mysterious inner knowledge that we, as dudes, will never understand. However, we can use it to learn. If she starts laughing at your pathetic male attempts to dress the little dudette, that's okay. Just remember that you can always pick out some really awful clothes for the little dudette, take her out in public, and then tell everyone her mom picked her outfit.

See, now you've both learned something.

daddy
day care

"i want my mommy!"

Here's where we get all serious for a minute. For a lot of dudes, the responsibility for a kid ends once they get their partner pregnant. After that, they think, it's a woman's job. We, rather obviously, disagree with that.

It's the responsibility of every dude with a kid to spend as much time as possible with that kid. She's going to need you in her life, and you're going to find that you need her just as much, if not more.

Barry: *When we adopted our fourth child, the youngest, she was only three days old. I stayed home with her for a week, just me, while my wife had to go to work. It was hard, no question about that. I had to learn on the job how to take care of an infant girl. But I wouldn't have missed it for the world. Really. I got to be there for her and hold her and gaze into her eyes, and, of course, change all of her diapers. For almost a week, I was her whole world. And that's a wonderful thing. We really bonded with each other. What I remember most about that first week is her being in the child sling strapped across my chest, sleeping soundly. It was just soothing for me to feel her there because I could tell that she was breathing and happy, and I didn't have to worry about anything. I also took time off to be with the other kids* *we adopted, but, because they were older, it was a little bit easier to take care of them.*

People say that there's a special bond between mother and child because she carried the baby for nine months inside her body. And, yeah, that's probably true. We couldn't say for sure. Richard only looked pregnant.

Richard: *When our youngest was about a month old, I took over caring for him the entire day, seven days a week. That was a shock. I'd only ever cared for our older boys when they were, in fact, older. I never knew how much harder it would be with such a little dude. He ran me ragged. So ragged, in fact, that when he took a nap, so did I. But, still, it was great to have all that time with him. Now, when he skins his knee, he cries out for daddy. I like that.*

I Wanna Play!

So your little dude is home and you're ready for some real, quality daddy time with him, and what's the first thing you bring out? If it's a regulation NFL football, then you've got some serious thinking to do about playtime, dude. Your little dude is simply not ready for that sort of thing.

Check out any toy store and you'll see what kinds of things would be safe for his age. Make sure you look at the age-appropriate rating of the toy before you bring it home for the little dude. Because, the thing is, no matter how much you want him to start tossing the football around, it's just not possible. There's a reason those toys have an age label on them. Kids don't come out of the womb ready to run and play. For that, you want monkeys. Monkeys are fun. But they're not little dudes.

If you want something to do in the early days that will make him happy, and be good for him, too, we've got a fun idea. While the little dude is awake, set him on his stomach on a blanket spread out on the floor, and gently rub your fingers up either side of his spine. This will help activate muscles around and near his spine, making them stronger and getting them ready to start supporting his weight when he's ready to move about. That's in the future, though. There's still a lot of time between then and now.

At one month old, your little dude will love a soft rattle and soft books with high-contrast patterns. But you don't need that stuff to have a good time with your little dude. Because the best toy you'll ever give the little dude is your own bad self.

> **Barry:** *My favorite thing to do with my little dudes, even now when the two oldest ones are almost teenagers, is to sneak up on them and tickle them mercilessly. No toys needed, just nimble fingers.*

All it takes is time, a little creative effort, and a willingness to have fun, and you can have a great day with the little dude.

the dude's guide top 10 list of things to do with your little dude or dudette

1. Play peek-a-boo until he gets tired of it, or your hands fall off. Repeat.

2. Do what *she* wants to do, not what *you* think she should want to do.

3. Listen with your ears and your eyes.

4. Enjoy walks in the outdoors as often as possible. And both of you should wear sunscreen.

5. Find her tickle spot.

6. Let him see you doing the right thing.

7. Lie down on your back, with her on your chest, and just enjoy.

8. Watch *Winnie the Pooh and Tigger Too*.

9. Discover the joys of reading with him.

10. Laugh with her, love her, and hold her tight.

Grab Time by the Hand and Never Let Go

Time is more than just the ticks on your wristwatch. Or, for you younger dads, the pixels on your phone as the digital numbers wind ever upward.

Time isn't just a measure of moments gone past, or moments yet to come. Time is a smile. Time is a finger gripped by a tiny hand. Time is lurching away, and —

Hey, sorry if we were getting a little too sentimental. The fact is, time doesn't only let us see the pleasant things, but the unpleasant, too. Some of the stuff stinks (both literally and figuratively), but it's stuff you will want to be there to experience.

Which brings us to that old cliché. Time passes much too quickly. First they're babies. Then they're kids. Then they're graduating from high school, etc., etc. Time isn't something you can go back and look for after it's passed. When it's gone, it's gone.

We've said it before, but let's make this plain. Take time for your little dude. Take time to be with him, and take joy in all his awesomeness.

Barry's friend Kevin got lucky. He got laid off. No, it wasn't lucky that he no longer had a high-paying Wall Street job, running a division of a big bank. He got lucky because he realized that getting laid off would pay him something he hadn't had before: time.

> **Kevin:** *My first week after being laid off was horrible. Really just incredibly unpleasant and nasty. It sucked. Big time. I was crabby and mad and mean and worried and ornery and just about drove my wife crazy.*
>
> *The week I got laid off was the last week of her maternity leave. She was getting ready to go back to work, thank goodness. Fortunately, she had a pretty high-paying job, which would at least keep us going until I could get back to doing what I was born to do: work hard and bring home the bacon.*
>
> *Our son Luke was about four months old at the time. We'd arranged to pay a friend to look after him until*

he was six months old and we could enroll him in the day care we both liked. With me out of work, though, I suggested to my wife that it made more financial sense for me to look after him than to pay our neighbor to do that.

My wife thought I'd gone nuts from not working, but I knew I could handle it. I mean, I ran a highly successful division of a large bank. How hard could it be looking after one little kid?

After my wife stopped laughing, she agreed that it probably made financial sense for me to take care of Luke. At least for a little while. I decided to think of it as a vacation. My first in a long time.

On my wife's first day at work, I can't tell you how horribly out of place I felt. There I was, standing in the doorway, holding our child, as my wife drove off to her office.

I can't imagine I was too much fun those first couple of days, but Luke never complained. That is, I don't think he ever complained. Maybe that yelling I took to be him telling me he was hungry was really him complaining about my bad attitude.

That started to change, slowly. Taking care of the kid was a lot harder than I thought it would be. I mean, when he was awake, I had to be focused on him all the time. I couldn't get a coffee break or pass him off to an assistant. It was rough.

Once I started napping when he napped, I began feeling better and probably just repressed all that stuff about being out of work. My attitude improved. I found myself looking forward to seeing Luke in the morning, taking him to the local bookstore for story time (where I got stared at by all the mothers), and doing all the fun things I got to do with him.

I won't say it was easy, because it wasn't. But I wouldn't trade that time I spent with Luke for anything.

We played "summer camp" at home. Making crafts by playing with scratch paper and glue. I was never much of a craft person growing up, so I didn't have much to go on, but I found that Luke loved playing with — and ripping up — paper. Who said crafts had to be useful? Or good? We just had fun.

Yeah, I lost my job, and, yeah, that sucked. But there will always be some job out there for me to find. Every day my kid gets older, and once time is lost, you can't get it back. I'd much rather have "Great Dad" on my tombstone than have it say something about how I was a hard worker.

Not every dad is as lucky as Kevin. Not every dad will get the opportunity to spend substantial quality time with his new little dudette. Not every dad can watch as she takes her first step, or stands for the first time, or cruises along the sofa and gets a surprised look on her face when she discovers that the sofa ends.

But every dad can make sure that the time he does have with

his child is meaningful. Don't try to squeeze her in between reading a prospectus and writing up a report. Laugh with her. Snuggle with her. Talk to her and listen to her babbling. Most of all, just be with her.

Take the time. Make the time.

You'll be glad you did.

the dude's guide top 10 list of things NOT to do with your little dude or dudette

1. Check to see if the old wives' tale is true about babies always landing on their feet.

2. Get front-row seats to the Led Zeppelin, White Stripes, Guns N' Roses reunion concert.

3. Make your wife cook, clean, and feed the little dude, and then haul him with you to the golf course and country-club bar for the weekend.

4. Find a panther to see if anything about *The Jungle Book* is true.

5. Teach her to swim by throwing her off the high dive.

6. Have his name engraved on the bar stool next to yours.

7. Invite him to join you in a father-son game of knife juggling.

8. Bring him to Mt. Everest for playtime. Need we say more?

9. Take his last bottle of breast milk when those Cheerios start calling your name.

10. Give him a coupon for "minors day" at the tattoo parlor.

up for grabs

magpies aren't the only ones attracted to shiny objects

Babies will put anything in their mouths. When we say anything, we mean anything. If it will fit in their mouths, great. If it's too big to completely fit in their mouths, well, they'll just start shoving as much of it as possible in there and drooling all over the rest. We're talking fingers, hands, toes, feet, and bowling balls, just for a start.

There's also pennies, and all sorts of loose change. Paper clips. Pens. Knives that aren't locked up. Television remote controls. Cell phones. Smartphones. Cameras. Your iPad. Just about anything. And, for some reason, if there's something electronic that won't take well to being dunked in spit, well, that's gonna be the little dude's favorite chew toy.

Also, babies like to grab just about anything. Once they do, of course, then they remember the whole mouth thing. But you need to be careful about the grabbing. Little dudes and dudettes love the shiny stuff. They especially love to grab earrings already in ears. And then they *pull*. Which hurts. A lot.

They will also grab and pull necklaces, bracelets, nose rings, belly rings, toe rings, ring rings, and watches. Then they remember that whole mouth thing, and it's open wide.

Barry: *One day, my sister-in-law, who was holding my youngest daughter, said, "Hey, where'd my earring go?*

I must have lost it." I suggested that it might have fallen to the floor.

My wife said, "Well, you'd better find it. I don't want our daughter putting it into her mouth."

At just that second, our little dudette went "blerg" and stuck her tongue out. Of course, the earring was sitting on top of her tongue. We got lucky that time.

Richard: *My little contribution is for all the dads out there with bad eyesight. I wear glasses, and I have kids. Sometimes that's not a good combination.*

Once, when I was holding my middle son, he reached up, and I must have had a complete brain fart or something, because I leaned down to smile in his face. He promptly grabbed my glasses and whipped them over his head. They flew to the floor and broke. I had to wait until the next day before I got a new pair of glasses and could see again.

And back to the title of this chapter. Grabby little hands can also be grubby little hands. Yes, kids' hands will get dirty. Very, very dirty. And the older they get, the dirtier they will get. So it's a good idea to keep some hand sanitizer at strategic points around the house, because you never know when you're going to need it.

you scream, i scream (not)

notes on calming your baby – and yourself

Now that your little dudette is home from the hospital, your life is about to get much, much louder. One of the defining characteristics of a baby is that she will scream. And scream. And scream. And scream some more, just for good measure.

She will scream when she's tired, when she's hungry, when she's cranky, when she's bored, when she's hurt, or when she just wants something to do.

Just because she's screaming and crying, though, doesn't mean there aren't a number of things you can do to try to calm her down. Here are just a few ideas. It's not a comprehensive list, because we don't know your little dudette. You do, and you'll learn more about her as she teaches you.

When she's crying and screaming, you can:

- try singing and talking to her.

- rock her back and forth.

- play with her.

- hold her gently to your chest.

- give her a ride in the car.

- give her a warm bath.

If the little dude has been fed recently and still is crying, you might try giving him a good burp to make sure you get rid of any gas bubbles trapped in his stomach. A quick note about that good burp: It's really okay to just go to town on your little dude's back — just start whaling away on his back when you're trying to coax a gas bubble up and out. Not every little dude likes this sort of treatment, but if you can't get the burp out any other way, feel free to up the velocity. Now back to the screaming.

The most important thing to keep in mind when you're faced with a screaming little dudette is to stay as relaxed as possible and to smile a lot. The more relaxed you are, the easier it will be for her to relax. No, that won't be easy. Baby screams can be worse than the screech of fingernails on a blackboard or the sound of fork tines being scraped across a plate. But you can't allow yourself to become frustrated by her wailing. The most difficult time for you will be when you have tried everything you can think of, and she still won't stop screaming. We still have horrible nightmares about that sound and the mounting frustration we felt when she wouldn't stop crying.

If your frustration starts turning into anger or panic, it's time to step away. Get your partner or someone else you trust to hold her and calm her down. Sure, a new face might make her feel a bit cranky, but it's worth it if handing her off will give you the chance to calm yourself down. If it's just you and the little dudette, then put her in her crib and step outside her room for a bit. Get some distance. Even if you do get angry, you need to know that you can *never, never, ever* shake your little dudette. Shaking an infant can cause brain damage, blindness, or death. Let us repeat: Do **not** ever shake your little dude or dudette.

> **Richard:** *If you get nothing else out of this chapter, please make sure you learn and live this piece of advice: don't take the screaming personally. She really isn't out to get you, just like my little dudes weren't intentionally trying to aggravate the heck out of me. It's just that crying is what babies do. I had to learn to take a mental step back and relax. The hardest thing for me to do was to keep calm when my dudes started screaming while we were in the car, and I couldn't stop to console them. I had to just let them cry. They were safe in their car seats and there was nothing physically hurting them, so it was okay. Annoying as all heck, but okay.*

Remember, screaming might just be the only way your little dude knows how to communicate. It's not like he can engage you in a little light banter to pass the time. He can't do anything else. It's your job to learn how to understand his needs and even predict them before he starts squalling. And dudes are good at their jobs, right?

Which means you're going to have to become really, really good at something that you, as a dude, have avoided for a long time. You'll have to start communicating. About your (shudder) feelings and your little dude's feelings. You're going to feel like you're drowning at first. But remember this:

Communication isn't just a river in Egypt.

No, wait. That's not how that goes. Just wait a tick. Ummm . . .

Communication is the medium and the message?

Nope.

Wait. We've got it this time. (We actually looked it up on Google, but we're pretty sure that if you can do it in under five seconds, that counts as knowing these days. Right?)

Communication is ~~not~~ a two-way street.

Whew. Thought we'd never get that one across.

See what we did there? Some bad communication where you didn't know what we were trying to say, but you kept on reading anyway? (We hope!)

Yeah, that's communication, and it was ugly. And we're talking communication between two adults. Now imagine you're trying to communicate with someone whose idea of eternity was the five minutes between when he peed and when he got a new diaper.

Let us be blunt about this: babies can't think. It's not that they won't think, like some teenagers we could name, but just that they don't have the physical equipment, the life experience, or the framework for interpretation that allows for cognition. (Sorry, we just liked the sound of all those long words.)

Anyway.

Even though babies can't think, they still experience this whole new world that keeps shoving itself into their faces. And that experience causes reactions. Which, in turn, causes your little dude to express himself in the only way he knows how. By screaming. At top volume. In an enclosed space.

Continued on page 162.

what to do when the little screaming banshee belongs to you . . .

The most horrifying stories don't contain a knife. Or a mask-wearing psycho. Or razor gloves. Or amorphous, invisible blobs on a green-lit home video. No. The absolute worst, most appalling stories involve a baby. A screaming baby. And worst of all (imagine the sound of an ominous piano riff and a creaking door) . . . there's no way out!

And even worse than the worst is when it's *your* little dude doing the screaming. Don't panic. We're going to walk you through a captive-audience scenario and give you tips about what you can do so that your baby — and the folks around him — don't have to suffer.

If you're on a plane or train and your little banshee won't stop crying . . .

1. The first thing you should do is to apologize to the people sitting around you. Let them know that you understand it's bad and that you're sorry. Then, get to work.

2. Intake: Check to see if he's hungry or needs a bottle. Being the prepared dad you are, you're going to have this sort of stuff handy so whip out some grub and give it a try.

   a. If the screaming is happening during takeoff or landing, it might be because her Eustachian tubes are blocked and she can't equalize the pressure in her inner/middle ear. Try to get her to swallow, which can do the trick. Or physically manipulate her jaw open and shut, which can cause the Eustachian tubes to open wider and allow the pressure to equalize.

3. Output: Check his diaper to see if there's anything in there that shouldn't be. Also, check to see if he's got a wicked diaper rash. Change the diaper. If his bottom is red, slather on some zinc oxide to protect the raw skin.

4. Output 2: He might need a big burp. Put him on your shoulder and work that burp up and out. It might turn out that he needs some more chest time, in which case, you can gradually decrease the force of the back-whaps and throttle down to pats to calm him.

5. **Output 3: Think back. Has he pooped recently? If not, he might be constipated.** This isn't going to be fun, but it can work well. Take him to a place where you can lie him down and open his diaper. Take out a thermometer or something similarly shaped, lube it up, and gently insert it into his anus, then gradually put pressure on the anal walls. This can stimulate him into pooping. If he hasn't done it in such a long time that it's causing him distress, you could be in for an explosion. Duck and cover.

6. If the screaming has nothing to do with the input/output, it might just be because your little dudette just wants to scream. She might be bored. Distract her by bringing out the favorite toys you brought with you. Be sure to have some new toys as well for just such an emergency.

7. Swaddle the little dude by tightly wrapping him in a blanket. This feeling can simulate the safe sensation of being in the womb. Babies like it. While swaddling the little dude, try gently rocking him back and forth. While you're rocking him, try putting a blanket over your heads to try to lower the light level and maybe decrease the noise.

8. If you're the digital-dad type, you're not going anywhere without a smartphone or a tablet. Try playing some music or a brightly colored movie for him. Or sing softly to him yourself. Again, the object is to distract him so that he forgets he's bored or upset.

9. Put the little dudette on your shoulder, rock her up and down while patting her back, and walk up and down the aisles. Yeah, you're spreading the volume to more people, but babies love the sensation of moving, as long as they're still close to their dad or mom.

10. Finally, one reason a lot of little dudes scream and cry a lot is something called colic. We're not sure what causes it and there's really nothing you can do to alleviate it, other than to treat the screaming symptoms by trying to soothe your baby in any way you can. (We hear swaddling helps.) If you know your little dude is colicky, it may be best not to fly with him until the condition dissipates.

As bad as the sound of a screaming baby is, it's not going to kill anyone. Folks will usually understand that it's not anyone's fault, just bad luck. They'll just want to see you step up to the plate to get your bundle of joy to be joyful again.

And then, every once in a while, he'll smile the most heartbreaking smile in the history of history, making all the drama worthwhile and giving you something to hold onto the next time the screams start back up again.

Remind yourself that it's your little dude just talking to you.

But, as we stated earlier, communication is a two-way street. By that, we mean that your little dudette is going to scream and throw fits, but you're also going to have to try to get stuff across to her as well. And it's a good bet that she won't understand anything you say to her, even if you phrase it in words of one syllable or less. With one minor exception, because this is a word you're going to say more often than you ever wanted to.

That word?

Yep. It's no.

"No, don't do that!" "No, watch out for that vase falling on your face!" "No, don't swallow that penny!" "No, don't grab Daddy's scissors!" "No, don't try to eat the handle on the grocery cart!" No. No. No. A thousand times no.

Even if you make up your mind before the little bundle of spit is born that you'll never say no to him, odds are pretty good that you'll still wind up using the word. A lot.

> **Richard:** *John and I have been friends since we both were in fourth grade. And if ever there was someone more resistant to having kids than me, it was John. And here he is with four beautiful kids, one son and three daughters. And a story to tell:*
>
> **John:** *I tried. Lord knows I did. I'd seen those mothers at*

the mall. You know the ones, who keep yelling "no" at their kids. It could get so ugly. With the number of times these kids got to hear their mom and dad yelling no at them, I'm surprised it's not the first word a lot more kids say.

Once I knew I couldn't escape the whole fatherhood thing, once I realized with joy that I would become a father, I had a long talk with my wife. We decided we weren't going to become those people. We weren't going to be yelling "no" at our baby all the time.

Starting off, it wasn't hard at all. Michael was a newborn baby and didn't do much more than cuddle and eat and sleep and poop. Then he started reaching for stuff like glasses and earrings or mustaches. And that got a little harder.

We'd tell Michael things like, "We don't do that, honey." We'd make sure we didn't use "no." And it worked. For a while. After all, who could say "no" to a face like that? We couldn't.

But there were a couple of problems with that. For one thing, Michael was a baby. He couldn't think. And when we were talking to him in complete sentences, explaining that he should mind his manners and not reach out to tip over the glasses on the dinner table, it wasn't really getting through. I kept imagining things from Michael's point of view — to him, I probably sounded like an adult in a Charlie Brown cartoon. "Wah wah wah. Wah wah wah. Wah waaaaahhh."

The other problem was that we sometimes had to act quickly. If Michael was reaching for something dangerous and we weren't close enough to grab him, we didn't take the time to think up something that gently explained to him the correct action. We just shouted and leapt. So, despite all our best efforts and good intentions, we did end up saying "no" pretty often.

Okay, so what impact does our saying "no" have on little ones? Does it mean that it will be the first word they gurgle? Well, it ain't necessarily "no." In a 2011 survey of 1,100 moms, the Web site CircleOfMoms.com found that the most common first word babies said was "Dad," or some variation thereof. (But of course it was.) It turns out that "no" came in as the seventh most common first word among the responding mothers. Right before "cat" and right after "ball." The word "Mom," or some variation of it, came in second.

The fact that "no" places in the top ten tells us all a little something about how often we say that word to our infants.

We've said it before and we'll probably say it again (because we're not the type of folks to throw out a good phrase just because it's not original, or not amusing, or not spelled right), but listen up anyway. Babies are sponges.

No, we don't mean that babies can absorb sticky spills on the kitchen counter. For that, we use the baby's diaper. Before he uses it. No, what we're talking about, really, is that little dudes and little dudettes are always paying attention. To *everything*. They can't help it. The world is so new and so loud and so bright and so grabbable and smells so strange, it just can't be ignored. They want to experience it all.

Every time you talk, it's only adding to the eventual word bank your little dudette will be using when she finally gets the physical dexterity necessary to start talking back. The joys you're going to experience once she does start talking, and the number of times you'll hear "no" coming out of her mouth in an ever-increasing number of ways, are stories for another book.

Suffice it to say, what you say now is something you will hear back in a very short while. But, until then, communication with your little dude is going to be frustrating. You need to get used to that. You also need to get used to the idea that you're going to have to do most of the work if you want to learn to understand each other.

The best way to get through to your little dude is to realize that he doesn't understand you (but will store away what you said for later use, remember?), and to just talk to him in a soothing, soft voice. Hold him close to you and let him feel the rumble in your chest as you tell him about your day, or ask him what he had for lunch and if there's any of it left.

Touch and tone are two very important things that you'll need to master if you're going to get something across to your baby. A soft touch and a gentle caress, a soothing tone . . . These can do more to calm down a crying baby than just about anything else.

Lately, there's been a lot of talk in parenting circles about the use of sign language to communicate with one's baby. Now, we can't speak extensively to the effectiveness of that, but we both used sign language to speak to our youngest kids. No, it wasn't the international sign language of the ticked-off driver. It was actual (sort of), for-real American Sign Language.

Both of us used a small number of pretty basic signs, Richard with Hyper Lad, and Barry with his youngest daughter. We taught them that if they put the thumbs and fingers of each hand together, then brought both hands together so their fingers met in the middle, it meant they wanted more. They also used the signs for eat and drink and please.

Richard, for one, was continually astonished that his little dude, who couldn't give you a verbal response other than a full-throated scream, could reliably ask for more to drink please, in sign language. Okay, sure, he probably didn't understand the words, but he knew that if he did certain movements, he'd get what he wanted.

Sounds like communication to us.

On another note, one of the best ways to communicate with your baby is to sing.

Which is good.

Barry will never — ever — be accused by anyone of having a scrap of talent for singing. But that didn't matter to his youngest daughter:

> **Barry:** *My little dudette loved the sound of my voice. I used to sing to her when I wanted her to sleep. I know my singing voice is terrible. But I also know that she loved to hear me sing. She'd smile in that way she had. I'd gently sing her a lullaby, and before I knew it she'd be drifting off to sleep.*

Which is wonderfully, amazingly good news for you. You've officially got our permission to go all *American Idol* on your little dude. Even better, there are no judges, and no one's going to be voting you off the show. Just don't start bringing in backup singers or a live band. That kind of thing can really ruin the intimacy of the moment.

stuff you've got to have

our top 10 list

Throughout this book, we've mentioned essential items that no home should be without once your baby arrives. We got to thinking (always a scary thing — just ask our wives) that it might be good to do a Top 10 roundup of these items, with a few new must-haves added in. Part of the reason is that we love David Letterman. We really do. We decided that if we're going to do another Top 10 list, we might as well steal from the best and do one like Dave's. Eventually, you'll put together your own Top 10 list of the baby stuff you've got to have, but we sure wish someone had given us a head start on ours.

Without further ado and in no particular order, here are the things we think are indispensable.

the dude's guide top 10 list of stuff you've got to have

10. **A bunch of pacifiers, and a few leashes to make sure you don't lose the pacifiers.**

9. **Old-school cloth diapers, because they're so absorbent. They make great burp rags and are fantastic for cleaning up spills.**

8. **Diaper-rash cream and Cetaphil moisturizing lotion.** Both are great for protecting your little one's skin.

7. **Bibs.** These are necessities. We always had a bib around our little dudes' necks to keep their clothes as clean as possible for as long as possible. We think the record for remaining clean and undrooled upon was 73 seconds, but it was a long 73 seconds. We suggest using cloth bibs, simply because they're softer, but plastic bibs are much easier to clean.

6. **Used-diaper disposal.** You're going to need a waste-disposal container to get rid of dirty diapers before they reach their final resting place in the outside trash. Make sure the container is out of the way and will keep the odor sequestered from the rest of the house.

5. **Saline and suction bulbs.** When little dudes get a cold, they can't really blow their own noses, so you have to clear it for him. The best thing to use is a suction bulb and saline water. You squirt a little saline water into his nose, which helps to unclog it, and then you use a different suction bulb to suck out the saline and snot. It's kind of disgusting, but it does help a lot.

4. **A backpack.** Yes, you absolutely need one. Not a made-for-a-woman diaper bag, but a backpack. Keep it by the door, stuffed with the things you need, so you are ready for any trip.

3. **A child-safety seat.** Getting one that you can pop out of the car is a necessity. These things are so cool. You can buy a system that works together with a stroller. The car seat snaps into a base in the car. Then, when you get where you want to go, you just take the seat out of the car base and lock it into the stroller. This is a great way to go, especially when the little dude is asleep and you don't want to wake him up.

2. **The BabyBjörn® infant carrier.** We're not normally inclined to endorse products by name, but with this one we just couldn't help ourselves. The BabyBjörn infant carrier is absolutely fantastic. You strap it around your back and slip the little dude into a carrier in the front. It's not too tight, and babies love it. You have your hands free, and the little dude is safe and secure — and best of all, close to you.

1. **Travel-sized packs of hypoallergenic baby wipes.** These little beauties can be used to clean up the little dudette or any sticky mess she leaves behind. They're also good as wash cloths for your hands before you pick up your baby.

20

splish, splash,
I was
takin' a bath

washing and drying

Bathing a little dude is not all fun and games, especially when you first get him home and give him his first few baths. The thing about it is that even though little dudes just came out of a liquid-filled womb, they're still not used to being taken from the dry world and put into a place where there's water all around them. So, he might be just a little bit cranky.

Here's the good news. As we said in a previous chapter, if you keep his genitals clean and do a good job of washing them off every time you change his diaper, there's no reason he has to have more than one or two baths each week during his first year.

The bad news, though, is that when he does have a bath, you can't just draw some water in the bathtub and then throw the little dude in there. Giving a little dude a bath takes work and preparation.

The first thing you've got to decide is where to give him his bath. You could buy a little plastic tub that you place in the sink. You fill that tub with water (more on that in a minute) and then do all the work standing at the sink.

> **Barry:** *Personally, I prefer bathing my little dudette in a bathtub rather than in the sink. By keeping her as close to the ground as possible, there's less chance of a fall.*

Of course, if you choose the tub, you still can't just throw him in there. You need some sort of device that will restrict his movement a bit and ensure his safety in the tub. There are all sorts of things you can use, and most of them are for sale at various baby superstores. What we recommend, though, is a giant sponge, about two feet long, that has a body-shaped depression in it, with a raised edge all around. This thing is fantastic. You can fill the tub with a couple of inches of water, which gets soaked into the sponge. This ensures that the little dude's back is getting wet and warm, while he becomes used to being in the tub.

Once you've chosen the place where you'll be giving the little dude his bath, then you need to get that area ready. You can't just turn on the water like you would for your own shower. There's a system. Before you begin with any baby bath, you need to make sure your water heater is set to no more than 110 degrees Fahrenheit. You'll have to do this at your water heater, which is probably out in your garage. That way, you won't scald your little dude.

First, turn on the cold water, and then turn on the hot water. You want to get a water temperature that feels warm on the inside of your wrist, which is more sensitive to temperature than your fingers. Remember, the little dude's not used to much in the way of temperature variations, so take it easy on him.

When you've got the temperature just right, then start filling the tub, whether you use the small plastic tub or the sponge or some other method. Do **not**, however, leave your little dude in any bathtub all by himself. While the tub is filling, make sure that you have all the items you'll need for the bath right beside you, so you won't have to go anywhere.

This is a checklist for what you'll need for his bath:

- very gentle baby soap

- a washcloth

- a small, waterproof toy for him to play with

- a dry, hooded baby towel

- your smiling face

The soap needs to be as gentle as possible, so as not to irritate his skin. The hooded baby towel is great for keeping him warm after his bath, and your smiling face will show him you're having a good time, which will help him to have a good time, too.

Speaking of which, this is a good time to repeat something very important: *never, never, ever* leave your little dudette alone in the bath. If the phone rings and you've got to answer it, or if someone knocks at the door and you feel that you must see who it is, you *take the little dudette with you*. No ifs, ands, or buts. We think it's always better that you get a wet shirt and have some water drip on the floor than to take the chance of leaving your little dudette alone in the bath.

Once you've got the little dudette in the water, you should allow her time to get used to it. Smile and play with her, and maybe use the washcloth to drip some water on her body so that she's not surprised by it. Then start getting her more wet.

The best way, we think, to bathe your little dude is to start at the top. Get his hair wet, and then use a little soap to clean it. Then use the washcloth to rinse it clean. Repeat this process over the rest of his body. When you get to his penis, testicles, and butt, clean him the way you would when you change his diaper. Lift his butt up, and then wipe all around with the soapy washcloth, making sure to get everywhere.

You'll also need to do a little special cleaning of the tip of the little dude's penis. Here's the 411 on that. As we mentioned in an earlier chapter, if he's been circumcised, the head of his penis will not be protected by the foreskin. And, because he's in a diaper all day, sometimes the rest of the skin on the penis will get pushed up around the head. If this happens, it can lead to the skin sticking to the head of the penis. You need to make sure that you softly pull back all the penis shaft skin from around the head and clean that area thoroughly and gently.

If you've got a little dudette, the same principle applies. That is, just like changing her diaper, you need to make sure to wash her from front to back, from vagina to anus, never the other way around. Also, remember to pull back all her skin folds and to clean out all the nooks and crannies by gently wiping.

Once you've bathed your little dude as much as possible, lay out the towel on the floor behind you and gently lift him from the tub and onto the towel. Put the hood over his head so he doesn't get cold, and then wrap him in the towel part. Probably the best place to dry him off is on your lap, so be prepared to get wet. We really do think it's a good idea to get a hooded towel. It's the same principle as going out in the cold and remembering to wear a hat; most of the heat in your body leaves through the top, that is, your head. A hooded towel helps to keep the heat inside where the little dude wants it.

things that go burp in the night

feeding someone who thinks oatmeal is spicy

Breakfast, lunch, and dinner. Pretty soon you'll be able to remember those quaint times when food was only on the menu three times a day, instead of every two frikkin' hours of every single day, twenty-four hours a day, seven days a week, four weeks a month. Well, we think you get the point.

You and your partner should have already decided the first of the many big food questions: bottle or breast. If you chose breast, well, you're in for both an easier and a harder time.

If your partner is breast-feeding, it will be up to you to take on a supportive role, since you, obviously, can't actually feed the little dudette. You will, however, be expected to do just about everything else, and, basically, anything your partner asks you to do. And she will ask you to do stuff. The minute you slack off, you will hear something along the lines of "I *have* to feed her. *You* don't do anything!" And, yeah, it can get worse. Worse than a crying woman clutching a baby to her breast and berating you? Oh, yeah, it can. So, for all our sakes, help out. Do whatever needs to be done. You don't need the agita and neither does she.

Trust us, you'll need to have a lot of patience if your partner is going to breast-feed. Even though it's as natural as breathing, it can still be a lot of work and take a lot of time to get right. Of course, having just read that and prepared yourself for the hardest time ever, it'll turn out that your partner takes to it like a hog to slop (no offense to your partner, dude, it's just an analogy), and you'll probably think we're a couple of know-nothing idiots.

If you and your partner have decided to bottle-feed your baby, then welcome to the wonderful world of the all-devouring maw. Where the little dudette will, it seems, almost always be hungry, and you and your partner will have to satisfy her endless appetite. You can't just send your little dudette out for pizza.

The reason she's always hungry is that she's so small. Her stomach, unlike ours, is only large enough to hold enough food to satisfy her for about an hour to an hour and a half. After that, it's time for another feeding. Babies getting formula from bottles usually last a bit longer between feedings than do breast-fed babies, but it's only by a little.

If you go the formula route, you'll need to start experimenting. You'll have to find the right formula for your little dudette. It might take a while, as some babies react differently to different formulas. Speaking generally, though, it's best to choose a formula that comes in two forms — powdered and premixed, single-serve bottles — that have a significant shelf life. That way, when you travel, you can buy those premixed bottles, instead of trying to mix formula on the go.

You also could use the premixed, already liquid formulas. You can skip the whole mixing part, but you do pay a price for this convenience. Literally. The premixed formula is more expensive. Still, it is an option.

Unfortunately, you won't get the relative ease of feeding her only formula for all that long. There's actually a little progression that goes something like this: bottle (or breast) for about six months, then over the next year or so, you start gradually introducing jar food. Once the dudette is eating only jar foods, you begin to slowly introduce solid foods, and then, once she kicks jar food, she's eating what you eat.

That's the way it's *supposed* to work. But every baby is different. She will choose when she's ready for something new — it's not up to you, friend. Your job is to experiment. Once she's able to sit up on her own, you might try her on different jar foods. If she doesn't like one, wait a couple of days and then try another. Remember to try only one new food at a time, though. If she reacts badly, it may be due to an allergy. If you only use one new food, you'll know the exact food to which she may be allergic.

All right, dudes, we hear you saying, "So you've told us *what* to feed her, but *when* am I supposed to feed her?"

Good question. Here's the deal. When she first gets home, your little dudette is going to sleep a lot. And when we say a lot, we mean, like, between 16 and 18 hours a day. And when she's not sleeping, she's going to be hungry. This goes back to the whole "small-tummy-with-no-room-for-food" thing. You should try to stretch her feedings out, waiting a little longer between each feeding, so you can try to get her closer to eating at normal times (and sleeping at normal nighttime hours).

If you decide to go with bottles, you should probably buy a couple of different types and try them out on the little dudette. You will want to find the one bottle with which she's most comfortable and that produces the least air, so there's less burping. The reason we suggest that you buy a couple of different types to experiment with is that you will be investing in a dozen or so, and you wouldn't want to have to keep shelling out that kind of cash on a bottle that, it turns out, doesn't work well.

Now that you've decided to help bottle-feed the little dudette and you know when to feed her, here's a little tip on the whole process. Have you ever seen a medical show? You know how the doctors scrub up before going in to operate? Yeah, well, you need to show them they ain't got nothing on you. You need to be as clean as possible when you're making a baby bottle.

Wash your hands. Wash the area where you're making up the bottle. Wash the bottle. Wash the nipple. Wash anything that even remotely looks like it might be connected to feeding your little dude. You don't want to know the kind of germs that can grow in those nice warm places all full of germ food. You really don't. And you especially don't want those germs getting into your little dudette.

In addition, when you get ready to feed her, you'll want a clean bib (she will spill some) and a clean burp rag (well, as clean as those ever get, anyway), because she will spit up after eating. And, yeah, the stench of regurgitated (look it up) breast milk or formula does smell just as bad as you think it will. Possibly worse.

When your little dudette first comes home and is happily guzzling from her bottle, you might, at times, be tempted to vary her diet a little bit. Because, after all, who would want to subsist on the same thing for every meal every single day? As it turns out, she would. The formula is good for her. Not only that, but to her it tastes good. So, do *not* supplement her formula with any water, sugar water, or juice until your pediatrician has told you it's the right time.

Dinnah Is Soived!

All right, let's get to the nuts and bolts of bottle-feeding a little dudette. The first thing you have to do is to warm up the food. Make sure that you do not use a microwave to heat the bottle or any food you plan on feeding her. The reason for this is that sometimes microwave heating can produce super-hot pockets within the food, while leaving the rest of it just warm. It would be a bad thing for something so hot to come into contact with your little dudette's sensitive skin and mouth.

Seriously, don't use the microwave.

We've found that one of the best ways to heat the bottle is to warm up some water in a pan on the stove. Not boiling, only hot. Then turn off the heat and put the bottle in for a while to get the formula warm. Yes, this can take a while, which means that you need to have a good sense of her schedule, so you can start warming the bottle *before* she becomes a screaming ball of hunger.

Of course, if you want to go all high tech, that's all right as well. Hey, we're dudes. Who doesn't love high tech? You can buy an electric bottle warmer: just plug it in, slip the bottle inside the warming sleeve, wait a few minutes, and — presto! — you're ready to feed.

After you've warmed the formula, it's time for the big test.

Take the bottle from the warmer, put the cap over the nipple, and then shake it firmly to make sure that there are no hot pockets to burn her mouth and that the formula is evenly warmed. Then you need to put a few drops on the inside of your wrist, which, again, is more sensitive than your fingers, to see if the formula is just a little bit above body temperature. If it is, you're ready to go.

You need to get comfortable. Feeding time could take a while, since she's not used to eating. We've found that when she first gets home and is too young to sit up, the best thing to do is to put a bib around her neck and then cradle her in your nondominant arm. That is, if you're right-handed, hold her in your left arm. Rest her head against your chest, with her back along your arm. Make sure that her body is slanted up, so her head is higher than her legs. Position the bottle in the baby's mouth, and make sure that the nipple is filled with formula so there's no air in it.

Little dudettes, future connoisseurs that they are, tend to view feeding time as an opportunity to truly pig out and will try to slurp down as much as is humanly possible. Your job is to slow her down a little bit so she doesn't overfill her tiny stomach. Because, if that happens, well, remember what we said about the awful smell of regurgitated formula? If you let her eat too much, she'll be spewing most of it into your lap.

While you're feeding her, try to make it fun. Talk to her and make her comfortable, so she knows that eating not only tastes good, but is enjoyable for other reasons, too (like seeing daddy smile). That attitude will come in handy when you start introducing new stuff like . . . peas or carrots. One last thing:

When you're feeding her, it's crucial to support her head at all times. Her neck muscles aren't yet strong enough for her to keep her head up by herself. For most little dudettes, the whole weak-neck thing only lasts a couple of months.

In Some Cultures It's Considered a Compliment

About halfway through the bottle, it's time for what could be the funniest part of feeding. Especially if you're not the one feeding her.

There she is, your little dudette, the apple of your eye, this tiny bundle of love. And she lets out with the loudest burp you've heard since the last time Bubba came over and drained your final six-pack of Busch Lite. If you're not expecting it, that thing can knock you over.

But, humor aside, it is important that your little dudette has a good burp after each feeding, or she will become extremely cranky. And she will need to burp. In all that slurping down, she's also swallowing a lot of air, which leads to burping. Unfortunately for you, air won't be the only thing coming up. She'll also be spitting up some of whatever she just ate. Again, you need to be prepared and have the burp rag ready!

We recommend getting some of those old-school cloth diapers, as they're more absorbent than just about anything else we've found. You need to put the burp rag under her head and neck when she's feeding, then use it to wipe off her mouth about halfway through the feeding. You'll also do the same thing after she's had her fill.

As much fun as it is for dudes to burp as often and as loudly as possible, it's sometimes hard to believe that some folks have a difficult time bringing up a burp. Well, it's true. It's especially true of the little dudettes and little dudes. So, here are a few quick tips on how to get baby to burp.

Support her body upright so that the air in her stomach has a better path out the body, and hold the burp rag just below her mouth. There are a number of different methods to doing the burp, and you should experiment to find what she and you like best.

> **Richard:** *Personally, I liked to do the two-handed deal. I would prop my little dudes upright on my lap and hold them there with my right hand, which also held the burp rag, and then I'd pat them on the back with my left hand. That just seemed to work best for them.*

> **Barry:** *Bah! The best way I've found is to have her straddle my left leg, facing away from my body. I lean her forward and hold the burp rag in my left hand under her chin. Then I tap on her back with my right hand while gently bouncing her up and down with my left leg. I call this the Super Burp Technique. Patent pending.*

Like we said, you'll need to experiment. Each little dude and dudette is different, so have fun with it.

As she gets older, you'll find that your little dudette is sitting up, and you might be tempted, especially if you're really busy, to just prop the bottle somewhere so that she can feed herself. Not a good idea. She's going to wiggle around and knock things over, which can lead to a very frustrated little dudette. Additionally, it's not all that safe. You need to be there in case she starts to choke. Remember, she's an inexperienced eater and needs all the help she can get.

the dude's guide top 10 things seen while feeding a baby

1. It's a breast. Get over it.

2. Sharks, wearing the latest in dog-mimicry technology, circling the high chair.

3. Goo. Of all kinds, all shades, all consistencies. From and in every orifice, even the ones you don't want to think about while someone's eating.

4. Cheerios. So many Cheerios that you'll never want to see them ever again. And goldfish. The same thing for goldfish.

5. Massive spills from not putting the bottle nipple on the correct way. Take it from us, do not let his mom know that her precious milk was wasted because you spilled it.

6. The beautiful, blissed-out smile of a completely full baby, on the verge of sleep.

7. The beautiful, blissed-out smile of a completely full baby, on the verge of sleep, with copious gobs of spit-up rolling down his cheek and onto your best pants because you didn't want to wake him for a burp.

8. It's still a breast. You still need to get over it.

9. A gastrocolic reflex that's too quick to kick in. Either put up with the smell for the time it takes to finish dinner, or try to feed while also changing. And be sure to send us proof, because we're sure it can't be done.

10. A goldfish headed right for your eyeball, followed by a Cheerio, followed by prolonged laughter at the silly, silly face daddy is making.

Life After the Bottle

A few quick notes on post-bottle-feeding. If you're like most people, you'll probably use jars of baby food from the market. We're not going to get into the debate of whether it's better to make your own baby food or to buy prepared food. That's for you to decide. However, there are a few safety tips to follow no matter what kind of food you use.

Everything has an expiration date. Even breast milk stored in the refrigerator should be used within 24 hours. Baby food will go bad if it's not used by the date on the label. Especially if you have already opened the jar.

When you begin feeding your little dudette relatively solid food, make sure that you don't feed her straight out of the jar (no need for her to pick up your bad eating habits, dude). Seriously, put some spoonfuls of food into a bowl before feeding her. That way, you can save the food in the jar. If you feed her directly from the jar, the digestive juices in her saliva will start breaking down the food in the jar, leaving you with a slimy mess at the next feeding time. And considering what these baby foods look like when they're still fresh, that's saying something.

As with bottles, when you're heating relatively solid food, make sure to mix it up extremely well before feeding it to her, so that you remove any hot spots.

One final tip on feeding: You might want to brush up on Abstract Expressionist painting masters. Once you start feeding your little dudette solid foods, your shirts are going to start resembling the lesser works of Jackson Pollock.

pop's quiz

the food pyramid
or
"just pile it higher"

1 Your little dudette is screaming for something when you realize that she's hungry. You root though the fridge, but find that you're out of formula/breast milk. What do you do?

    A. Carefully warm up some of that organic vitamin D milk you've got in the fridge for just such an emergency.

    B. Panic! Grab the little dudette and put her in a sling as you run out the door to start hitting up the nice retired couple next door for formula.

    C. Figuring it's good enough for momma birds, so you can do it, too, you start chewing up that piece of ribeye really good. . . .

2 Your little dude is making really nice progress. He's still drinking milk, but has moved on to food that's more solid. Recently, he's gotten in the habit of needing a couple of jars of baby food at each meal. The fact that this is a relatively new behavior explains why you ran out of food on the one afternoon your wife left you at home with the baby. What do you do?

    A. Remember that baby food is only puréed adult food, so you scoop up some carrots and dump them in the blender for a long spin with very sharp blades.

    B. You've got a dog. Thumper's food is sort of semisolid like the baby food. The wife's not home. Who's to know?

    C. Still making like a momma bird, you chew up that piece of ribeye a little more thoroughly than you had planned.

3 Your sweet little dudette is a bundle of joy and cuteness. Most of the time. Her only problem seems to be that she is turning into a picky eater, one who will only tolerate certain foods. Only your wife knows which foods and the specific ways your daughter likes them — and she's away for the weekend. Your next move is to . . . get another good night's sleep, and soon. What do you do?

A. Look in the baby-food cabinet and see which food has the most jars, then hope a funny face is good enough to get her interested in eating.

B. Mix everything together in one big bowl, since it all goes to the same place anyway.

C. Scoop out a spoonful of baby food to taste while she's watching, thinking your daughter will imitate you and eat like a champ. You've never met a meal you didn't like. After you're done spitting and cleaning off your tongue with the steel wool, you look at your little girl with new respect.

If you answered A for these questions, we're proud of you. If you answered B, you definitely have more reading to do before you're ready to solo with your little dude or dudette. If you answered C, have some more puréed peas and carrots and call us in the morning . . . but by no means take charge of feeding your family.

hitting for the cycle

the learning curve

Baseball provides a great metaphor for getting to know your little dude so well that it'll lead to a much happier home life. In baseball, "hitting for the cycle" means hitting a single, a double, a triple, and a home run in the same game.

In parenting, hitting for the cycle means getting to know when and why your little dude wants to do certain things. In the beginning, it's going to be very basic stuff.

All people have natural bathroom, eating, and sleeping cycles.

What you need to do is to pay attention to your little dude's cycles as soon as he has his first day out in the big new world. If, for instance, you don't realize that he always wets his diaper during naptime and you don't change him first thing, then he might get diaper rash, which leads to cranky little dude and cranky big dude.

So here's the thing: if you're formula-feeding your little dude, his cycle will probably run something like what follows. However, again, let us caution you that this is just a rough outline, and it's up to you to fill in the details and maybe change the order.

- Sleep.

- Needs to have wet diaper changed.

- Eat.

- Needs to have pooped-out diaper changed.

- Play.

- Sleep.

- Needs to have wet diaper changed.

- Eat.

- Needs to have pooped-out diaper changed.

- Play.

We think you can get the rest of it from there. Once you learn his cycle, it'll make your life much easier. You won't be trying to play with him when he really wants to eat, or shoving food in his mouth when he really wants to sleep. As always, one important thing to remember is that your little dude could change his cycle at any time. This is another example of how you have to continue being observant, focusing on your little dude and his needs, even when you think you've got it down.

To close with another baseball metaphor, it's your turn at bat. Let's see how you do, slugger.

Be Gentle. It's My First Time.

Everything, and we do mean *everything*, is brand-new for your little dude when he is first born. For one thing, there's no more womb service. Hah! We've always wanted to use that pun.

Barry: *No, no, I didn't.*

Richard: *Well, I did. And, really, did you think we could get through this without me making that joke?*

Anyway, once the little dude is out and about, he's going to be doing some amazing things. Well, amazing for him, at least. And you'll want to pay attention. While some of these are medically and developmentally important, they're all pretty cool, so don't let yourself get distracted by doing too many chores or catching up on all the games you Tivoed.

For example, seeing some stranger on the street smile is no big deal. Seeing your little dude smile up at you for the first time? Priceless.

Here are some other milestones that you will experience:

Pooping. No, we're not suggesting that you celebrate the first of countless, smelly poops. However, as we covered in the chapter on changing the little dude, that first poop is going to be meconium: sticky, black, and ugly. But, once it's out of the way, it doesn't come back, so that's a plus. Just wipe, toss, and try to forget.

Umbilical cord. When the little dudette was in the womb, she was getting all her oxygen and food from her mom through the umbilical cord. When she was born, the obstetrician clamped and cut the cord. However, there's still a bit of it attached to the little dudette, and, yeah, it is kind of gross. However, it will fall off, normally after becoming hard and dark and shriveling up, between one and four weeks. The best way to deal with it is to roll the diaper down so that it's below the umbilical stump. That way it gets as much air as possible to dry out quickly. Put antibacterial ointment on the stump every time you change her, and check for any redness, oozing, pus, or swelling. If you see any of that, take her to your pediatrician. Also, make sure that you keep an eye on the stump, so that when it falls out, you can dispose of it. Fast. Faster than the dog, at the very least.

Smiling. Your little dude's first real smile should happen around the time he's four to six weeks old. It might happen a little earlier, though, so keep looking at him. And smiling. This might be a good time to remind you to get a camera and keep it handy. You'll want to be taking a lot of pictures of the little dude, and there's nothing more frustrating than seeing something amazingly cute, and then having to hunt for the camera. Capture those Kodak moments while you can, dude. Yeah, we know everybody's got cameras in their cell phones, but we do like single-purpose devices for the important things.

Laughing. It obviously goes along with the whole smiling thing and should happen around the same time. The first few times it happens, he'll probably be smiling in response to some sort of physical stimulation, like tickling. His sense of humor will take a little longer to develop and will, at first, be limited to responding to silly looks and pratfalls. Sort of like (now that we think of it) dudes of all ages.

Sitting up. By the time he's around eight months old, your little dude should be a muscle-bound strongman. Well, for an infant. His muscles will have become strong enough that he's able to hold up his head, roll over, and sit up. The good news is that your life just got much easier, as he'll be able to cooperate with bathing and feeding and all that other fun stuff. The bad news is that your life just got harder, because now he'll start squirming and wriggling like you won't believe during feeding, bathing, dressing, changing, and everything else you do with him. The plus-minus news is now you need to get out to the hardware store. That's always good because, hey, it's a hardware store, but you also need to buy all those cabinet locks and corner pads we discussed earlier in the book. Why? Look no further than the next paragraph.

Crawling. Most little dudes and dudettes learn to crawl between six and ten months old. Note that we said most. Others decide to slither like snakes, or slide along looking like they're low-crawling under the barbed wire of an army obstacle course. Some just skip learning to crawl altogether. It's not a big deal, though. The important thing is for him to learn to move around, and that will happen. It's also another great reason to have a camera or camcorder around.

Standing. He'll start to stand around the same time he learns to crawl. At first, he'll be pulling himself up on every couch or leg that he can get a good grip on. There are times when an upright moment will turn into a bit of a topple, but that's okay. We all learn from picking ourselves up and trying again. You'll also probably see him cruising. That is, supporting himself as he walks by grabbing onto the nearest chair or table. More camera time.

Walking. Once your little dude masters standing, it's only a matter of time and confidence before he's walking on his own. Most little dudes and dudettes take their first steps between nine months and one year of age. Your job is to make sure that he stays safe and happy while toddling around the house. Now is the time to do one more check of every room to ensure that all harmful chemicals and other materials are locked away and elevated beyond what the now-standing dude can reach.

Words. Your little dude probably will say his first recognizable word sometime between his ninth and 18th month, and, as we said earlier, it could very well be "no." However, before the first recognizable word in response to the correct stimuli, there probably will be lots of babbling. That's when you keep repeating "Daddy" to him every chance you get (remember that the little dude is a linguistic sponge who's soaking up everything he hears). You never know — with enough practice, it may be the very first thing he spouts. And since he's taking in everything, cut the four-letter words that can get him — and you — in trouble.

Prototyping the First Draft

Here's something you probably won't read in those *other* books on how to avoid being a bad dad. It's important, so listen up. You might want to start working on that apology right now.

No, not the apology you'll have to give your wife every time there's a fight. Or when a certain *glare* shows up, and you know better than to ask what's wrong. Or when she says she's *"fine."* Or . . . You know what? Let's just skip that part. It's possible we might be obsessing here a bit. No, the apology we're talking about is the one you're going to owe to your firstborn child. Even attaching a nice check to the inside of a card might not be enough. The reason? Well, no matter how well prepared you think you are, no matter how much advice you've sought, no matter how much you've practiced, you're going to mess up. Big time.

There's a saying among the big dudes and dudettes who have the unenviable job of planning how to win wars: no battle plan survives first contact with the enemy. And make no mistake, raising a child is war.

You're fighting against the outside world, well-intentioned idiots (family), the environment, and many others. There'll be times you'll be at (. . . ahem . . .) odds with your mate — and even with yourself.

We want to get this out there as plainly as possible, so listen up. With your first or only child, *you will be overprotective*. In addition, *you will make more mistakes with your first, since this is your first time up on the bull at this particular rodeo*.

It's all right. You wouldn't be a dude if you didn't screw up every now and then. When you look back, you're going to be more than a little sheepish about what went on during that first childhood. Don't worry. Everybody feels that way. It's cool. If we all could see the future as well as we can see the past, the stock market wouldn't be much of a gamble now, would it?

Don't sweat it. You might think that you haven't done enough. Or that you've done too much. Either way, it's all right.

Looking at the situation with a relatively unbiased eye, as long as your little dudette is safe, you're good. If it makes you feel better to babyproof the corners where the ceiling meets the walls, then go ahead and do it.

It's your first baby — go wild. Unfortunately for the little dudette, this is the time when you're learning what's necessary and what's not. And she's the one who gets experimented on, no matter how much you think you've got things figured out. Your carefully laid plans will fall to tiny pieces. Your expectations will die shrieking in a quick but messy explosion. Life, as is its wont, will get in the way.

Our friend Chris laughs whenever anyone asks him about how he was as a first-time father. Unfortunately, it's the sort of laughter you mostly hear from folks heading up the steps to that oddly tied loop of rope.

Chris: *Oh, man. I was Bad Dad. All the way.*

A few years after my son was born, when he still wasn't old enough to understand it, I started calling him the prototype. By then, he had a baby sister, but he was my first draft, my first experiment in how to be a father.

You know how on TV, whenever there's a scene set in a chemistry lab in a school, something always explodes during an experiment? My early experiments in fatherhood were like that. Stuff happened even though I had a good role model. My dad was great. But, you know, you always think you can improve on stuff.

If we can cut in here for a minute . . . Let us just tell you that Chris's son is a great young dude. He's not out breaking into cars or selling drugs or anything like that. He's a good kid, doing good in school, and doing good at home. And he certainly isn't sitting in front of his computer with our credit ratings on the screen and cackling gleefully. Nope. He's a good young dude, and all that talk about cornfields is just that: talk. Now, back to the story.

Chris: *Karen and I were what you might call a bit overprotective. Of everything. I mean, if someone breathed on his binky, we popped it out of his mouth, sterilized it with hot water, then did it again, cooled it down, and then glared at the offender before offering it back to our son. As he was growing, we wouldn't let him have any caffeinated drinks. No French fries. I mean, we even blended his baby food.*

By the time his sister came along, my wife and I had to go back to work, and that sort of stuff basically stopped. Our daughter was raised on grocery-store baby food and blown-off binkies. And she loved her drive-through hamburgers and fries.

But the problems didn't stop there for our firstborn. We didn't want him to feel like he was entitled to stuff, so we made him wait and work for things, like a portable music player. We told him that he couldn't have one that connected to the Internet, and he couldn't have one before a certain age. And we stuck to it.

Once he was old enough, he worked hard, and so we got him the music player. Well, we actually got two, because we also gave one to his sister. I mean, it was only a music player. Once our oldest had one, and we saw how he was using it, we realized that it was no big deal.

It kept going like that. Our oldest would have to work for something and wait, but our youngest just cruised along in her brother's wake.

Of course, you won't have to worry about that for a few years. While it's not yet your concern how to give an allowance to your little dude (since he can't even sit up on his own, much less start surfing through the seedier sites of the all-night shopping empire), Chris's story still has some instructive pointers we can all learn from. You'll start out full of plans and rules and expectations, and gradually you'll just see that your little dude or dudette will teach you how to parent. Without either of you even knowing it.

23

delegate,
schmelegate

somebody's got to do the dirty work . . . and it's you!

In the business world, the art of delegation is well regarded in an executive. After all, the top brass can't do everything. Finding the right people for the right job is a bit harder than just dishing out the stuff you don't want to do and making it someone else's job.

When you're a dad, though, delegation reeks of desperation. There are jobs no sane person wants to do when it comes to bringing up baby. Dirty jobs no one would film a television show about. Horrible jobs that will give you nightmares.

And you get to do them.

When facing that sort of overwhelming assault on your senses, the first thing you might think is, "HELP!" And, of course, the first person to come to mind who might be able to help and would definitely know what to do is . . . your mom. After all, she raised you, and you turned out all right. Right?

Let's stop you right there. No matter how tempting it might be, you need to get used to doing your own dirty work with the little dude. The little dude's grandparents might be all right with taking care of him for a little bit every once in a while, but don't count on them to pitch in 24/7. They did their time in the poop mines. It's your turn now. Time to man up, dude.

pop's quiz

what to do with your little dude when you just need ten minutes alone — is that too much to ask?

1. You need at least ten uninterrupted minutes to finish a presentation. (Six minutes to surf the Web. Two minutes to glance at e-mail, and a frantic last two minutes to actually do the work.) You've got the little dude with you for the day. What do you do?

   A) Do the work when it's his naptime, keeping track of him with a baby monitor in another room.

   B) Call your mom, begging for help and trying to convince her that if she hops on the plane *right now,* she'll be there in time to take over for an hour.

   C) Call your boss/client, and convince her that aliens have landed and begun a brutal occupation as they search for water to steal and brains on which to munch.

2. You want to get your three-month-old something to occupy her attention for a few minutes. Do you . . .

   A) get her a soft toy, covered in black-and-white geometric patterns, that has a squeaker in the middle?

   B) sign her up for the fast-pitch batting cages?

   C) have the complete works of William Shakespeare and Leo Tolstoy inscribed on her binkies for a little light reading?

3. You've heard that every little dudette should have a mobile gently twirling over her crib, because it helps her focus on new things and gives her something to watch as she falls asleep. What kind of mobile do you put over the crib?

   A) Remembering that most newborns can't distinguish colors very well, you purchase a black-and-white mobile that offers a number of different geometric shapes and plays a jaunty tune while turning and moving.

   B) You go to the garage and start hauling out the tools you inherited from Uncle Lefty and get to work, figuring it'll be a long while until she's able to stand up and touch it.

   C) You commission a new installation of a chandelier by renowned glass sculptor Dale Chihuly.

Choosing A as the answer to these questions shows that you've been paying attention, both to this guide and your little dude. Answering B is an indication that *you* shouldn't be left alone too long. If you answered C to any of the questions, your enthusiasm might have gotten the better of you. Dial it back a few settings and try again.

the dude's guide top 10 list of bad dads in the movies

1. Donny Berger, from *That's My Boy,* and Sonny Koufax, from its unofficial prequel, *Big Daddy,* are on this list because we're almost positive that Adam Sandler has never starred in any worse movies, and that's saying something.

2. Dr. Evil, from the *Austin Powers* movies, seems to be the type of dad you'd pay a lot of money to if only he'd go away. Maybe something along the lines of one miiiiiiiiiiillion dollars.

3. Satan/Lucifer, from the *Omen* movies — but, really, any movie in the devil-baby genre, because you can't have a devil baby without a devil-baby daddy. (A special nod in this catergory to the heartlessly ambitious father of Rosemary's baby.)

4. Peter McCallister, from the *Home Alone* movies, manages to go off on vacation and leave his youngest son home alone, not once, but twice.

5. Norman Osborn, from *Spider-Man*, goes out of his gourd, puts on a Power Ranger mask, manages to kill himself, and still forces his son, Harry, to carry on the family crazy business. And, dude, business is a-boomin'.

6. The Rev. Shaw Moore didn't want to be a bad dad. He did what he thought was right for his family and for the rest of the kids in his small town. How was he to know that it was time for the rise of skinny ties? How was Moore to know he'd soon be trampled beneath the juggernaut of charisma that is Kevin Bacon getting all *Footloose*?

7. Don Vito Corleone, from *The Godfather*, because . . . really? We really have to tell you why the Godfather is a bad dad? We'll give you a hint. It's not just because he makes offers you can't refuse, if you know what we mean.

8. Jack Torrance, from *The Shining*, if only because we know all work and no play makes Jack a dull boy, and he really knows how to put that special something into "Heeeeeere's Johnny!"

9. Mr. Wormwood, from *Matilda*, is possibly the most selfish person imaginable (topped only by his wife), in this movie adapted from the book by Roald Dahl.

10. Anakin Skywalker/Darth Vader, from the *Star Wars* movies, but more specifically *The Empire Strikes Back*, because his idea of bonding with his son is to invite him into the family business, cut off his hand, and throw him off a cloud city. Also, that breathing thing is just creepy. Remember: He finds your lack of faith . . . disturbing.

24

all pooped
out

the big finish
(or: you've only just begun,
but we're pretty much done)

Well, dudes, that's about it. We've passed the torch and shared all the wisdom that we know, and now we're all tapped out.

If you've read through the book, you should have a good, solid foundation you can use to build your own set of skills. A couple of years down the line, you'll probably find this book gathering dust in a corner of your house and think that you can't believe you ever needed to ask anyone any questions at all.

You'll be a dad, and dads know everything. We know ours did, at least until we hit around 14 or so, and then they became inexplicably dumb. Oddly enough, by the time we hit 23, they'd regained most of that knowledge. Strange how that works.

Speaking of knowledge, while writing this little book, we not only relied on our own experience (and that of our wives and friends), we also turned to a few books ourselves. The two we found most enlightening were *What to Expect the First Year* by Heidi Murkoff, and *Caring for Your Baby and Young Child: Birth to Age 5* from the American Academy of Pediatrics and editor-in-chief Dr. Steven P. Shelov. As we've said, our book is just a starting point. You're going to have to fill in the blanks. If you want to get more in-depth, we can't think of a better way than occasionally thumbing through these two tomes. They're daunting, but useful. You see, even your humble authors, paragons of knowledge and experience that we are, sometimes need a little outside help. You just might, too.

Being a dad is a bit like putting together a jigsaw puzzle. In the dark. While wearing mittens. It's damn hard work, but it's probably the most worthwhile thing you'll ever do.

It's also the most fun you'll ever have. And that's the important part. Once you've got the basics down, you'll be able to have fun with it all. You'll be able to relax, at least a little bit, and enjoy the little dude or dudette you're helping to raise.

So, enjoy it. We did. Now it's your turn.

Smart Dad or Slacker Dad? Which are you, dude?

Slacker Dad

We had the **baby.** Too late to back out now.

Smart Dad

You schedule tee time.

Bring the **baby** home.

You schedule lots of quality family time.

Shout to your wife: "Your turn!"

It's his first **poop** at home.

Man up, hold your breath, and change the diaper.

As you scrub up, you think about how to delegate all future diaper changes.

The little squirt squirts you.

Laugh and clean up the pee, covering the little dude with a diaper when you wipe down.

You turn down the baby monitor and catch a few more zzz's.

The baby wakes you in the middle of the night.

You stub your toe in the dark; cuddle the baby back to his nursing mom.

"Was it my turn to buy formula?"

Feed the baby!

Gently "sing" to the baby while checking the temperature of the warmed bottle.

You throw down a few pillows.

Babyproof your home.

Maybe one more coat of bubble wrap. Can't be too careful.

He's smiling. He doesn't care if the outfit's on backwards, so why should you?

Dress the little dude.

You've applied sunscreen to him and dressed him in a stylish onesie – he looks more dapper than you!

Run!

Your son writes his memoirs.

Smile!

Acknowledgments

No book ever is written by a single person. Even if it's only one author's name on the cover, the finished product is a team effort. With that in mind, Barry and Richard want to thank each other for all the mutual support, friendship, and encouragement. Thanks also to the little people who — Wait, why is that hook pulling us offstag —

On a slightly less cheesy note, we want to thank our wives, who had to put up with more than you readers will ever know. And that was even before we got the idea in our heads to write this book. Their love and belief sustained us during the long months when we thought no one would ever read this.

And, of course, we want to thank our little dudes and little dudettes — even though they won't let us use their names in the book, for fear that they will truly, literally die of embarrassment (they won't). They are wonderful, fantastic little people, and we love to be around them. And, when they're a pain in the butt, it's even better, because we're getting great material for the next book.

Our gratitude wouldn't be complete without also thanking Mary Baldwin and Charlotte Cromwell at Sellers Publishing, Renee Rooks Cooley for her proofreading, and Rita Sowins for her great design work.

Finally, a huge thanks to our editor, Mark Chimsky, whose hard work and dedication to making a really good book out of what Barry and Richard handed in was more than appreciated; it was inspirational. Thanks for taking a chance on us, Mark. And thanks to everyone at Sellers Publishing!